Human, Archhuman, Satanic

Contents

This book contains writings that address the topics most relevant to giving an idea of what the godless theology of Satanic System Ecclesia Luciferi is. Some of these writings are included on the Ecclesia Luciferi website: lucifernostrasalus.substack.com

These writings have been arranged in the form of a book in order to present in a more concise way the various cross-section of issues that the Ecclesia Luciferi system addresses and to look at them as a coherent whole.

Introduction

Lack of faith

It is not the belief in the non-existence of gods that is in question, but the complete absence of this belief. This complete denial of "the certainty of what is expected, the conviction of what is not seen" must come from the Devil himself. If nature is fallen because "sin came into the world", then the instinctive, natural rejection of faith in favour of reason must derive from original sin. It was Eve who first, enlightened by the Serpent, chose knowledge over blind faith. Yahweh God went into a holy rage when He learned that man had chosen Satan's truth over mindless belief in his dogmas. It is Satan who represents knowledge instead of faith; Satan lacks faith in god. Satan is the negation of god, he is the Anti-God. Satanism is the negation of religion, it is anti-religion.

Satanism is the enemy of any form of theistic manipulation of human emotions, subconscious and mind through fear of punishment in an imaginary afterlife, or false hope of a better life after death in flesh and blood.

The soul detached from the body does not exist. The mind detached from the corporeal brain does not exist. Evil from another world does not exist. Morality coming from the heavens does not exist. It is a falsehood based on delusion, accepted only on faith, this enemy of reason and knowledge. It is an undeniable fact that every holy book was written by man, every demon, angel, god or devil, every name written in these books was created by man.

All religions are the product of man. This is a fact. Gods without man would be nothing, they would cease to exist. Man without gods is and will continue to be man.

It took an Anti-god - Satan - to sow doubt in the false gods.

It took more than man inventing more and more religions out of ignorance and fear. It took a new man, let it be said, an Arch-human, stripped of all fear of eternal death and false faith, hope and love for sacred delusional lies.

Lack of reason

In the sixteenth and seventeenth centuries, writing such a book could be paid with one's life. Thanks to the Satanic Enlightenment, however, inquisitors possessed by holy madness no longer rule this world. Although there are still countries where the 'crime of blasphemy' is punishable by death. But that does not mean that religious fanatics would not want to rule again. Therefore, there is a need to write godless, blasphemous books

that challenge the theistic fallacy and show the absurdity of religious belief in general.

In order to dissuade as many people as possible from god and his imaginary kingdom.

Christians, those who truly believe in the truth of their bible, the one in which it is written that the universe was created about 6,000 years ago, created out of nothing by an invisible being not of this world, who created it in 6 days, believe fervently in the chaotic, ambiguous "prophecies" from which they read that soon their saviour will deliver them from this evil world and will burn the sinful world itself with fire. Moreover, their book exhorts them to hasten this doom:

"while you await and strive to hasten the coming of the day of God, which will cause the lit heavens to go up to destruction, and the stars to scatter in fire". - 2P 3.12

These people, wherever they gain even a share of power immediately try to write their

laws taken out of a Bronze Age book into the legislation of the country in question. Therefore, their "one and only" world view based on the delusions of ancient sheep herders affects all the citizens of a country. Regardless of whether these citizens share their view that the earth is flat or not.

Lack of religion.

Religion can be defined as a person's relationship to some deity and the divine realm manifested through faith and various religious rituals. Theistic religion is usually based on a belief in an invisible god or gods. And if these beliefs are derived from 'revealed truths' in sacred books, then there is no question here of any opposition to religious doctrines and divine laws. After all, these books were written down by divinely inspired prophets. And how does one know

this? These books say so and it must be taken on faith.

But knowledge is the opposite of faith. Where knowledge occurs there is no room for faith. For when you know something then you do not need faith. Faith disappears in the face of knowledge. That is why the preachers of faith hate knowledge so much. That is why knowledge is the enemy of faith. Knowledge comes from Satan.

That is why Satanism has nothing to do with religion and faith, because true Satanism is the opposite of religion. Satan is the powerful, primordial and most important symbol of rebellion against all authoritarianism, spiritual tyranny and blind faith in revealed dogmas, and true Satanism is the anti-religion. And this is what constitutes its truly diabolical power. Godless Satanism is a worldview that not only rejects belief in a god (like atheism) but is the very absence of all faith and is also a

fierce enemy of theistic superstition, that absurdity particularly pronounced in the Abrahamic religions. Satan is a symbol hated and feared by all those who base their worldview on blind faith and by all those who use the blind faith of followers to control them.

Satan represents the power of reason, scepticism, ungodly knowledge, and the sinful courage to acquire this knowledge, even in ways that are temporarily unacceptable to religious-minded people and temporarily forbidden. Satan, as a powerful symbol, has the infernal power to attract to himself all rebels who, after learning his philosophy, are able to be disenchanted and "born again" to an abundant life of flesh and blood.

After these words of introduction, let us look at the Devil, which, as we know, is in the details.

Lucifer

Luzifer - Franz von Stuck - 1890

The name Lucifer, which means light-bearer in Latin, causes anxiety and nervousness, at the very least, and often also fear and aversion, in the simple followers of the carpenter from Nazareth. To the more learned it appears as a symbol of godless enlightenment, sinful pride and blasphemous self-exaltation, that is the conviction that man does not need a god in

his life at all. And such an attitude is a mortal sin against the divine need for totalitarian absolute power.

The name was also known in the non-Christian world.

In ancient Rome, the name Lucifer was used to denote the planet Venus, or in more poetic terms, the god of the morning star, who was the commander of the stellar legions.

The Latin poet Ovid, in his first century epic Metamorphoses, describes Lucifer as follows:

„Aurora, watchful in the reddening dawn threw wide her crimson doors and rose-filled halls; the Stellaa took flight, in marshaled order set by Lucifer, who left his station last".

However, with the advent of Christianity, traditionally, what preceded Christian religious fantasies had to be distorted and disgusted. What was natural had to be

degenerated. And delusions had to be elevated to the status of revealed truth.

Christians, specialising in the manipulation and distortion of the old Hebrew scriptures in order to justify their made-up religion promptly began to use various texts from the Hebrew scriptures out of context, and present them as prophecies.

Thus the following passage from the book of Isaiah would describe Lucifer:

„How that thou didst fall from the heavens, Shining One, Son of the Dawn?

How didst thou fall to the earth, thou who didst conquer the nations?

Thou who spake in thy heart: I will ascend to the heavens; above the stars of God I will set my throne.

I will sit on the Mount of Meeting, at the ends of the north.

I will ascend to the tops of the clouds, I shall be like the Most High.

What do you mean? You have been cast down to Sheol to the very bottom of the Abyss!" Isaiah 14:12,15

And here is how the first line of this text reads in Latin. It is a passage from the Vulgate, the first translation of the Bible into Latin, which was produced in the 4th century c.e. The author of the translation was Saint Jerome:

*„quomodo cecidisti de caelo, **lucifer**, qui mane oriebaris corruissti in terram qui vulnerabas gentes."*

The Latin translation of this passage uses the name Lucifer explicitly.
Isaiah's text here parallels the words attributed to Jesus about Satan:

Then he said to them: "I saw Satan falling from heaven like lightning". Luke 10:18

Another Old Testament text that Christians unequivocally identify with Lucifer is this one from the Book of Ezekiel:

"Thou hast been in Eden, the garden of God; thy garments were all manner of precious stones: carnelian, topaz and jasper, chrysolite, beryl and onyx, sapphire, ruby and emerald; of gold were thy tumblers made, and thy ornaments were made in the day that thou was created. Next to the cherub who defended the entrance I have set thee; thou hast been on the holy mountain of God, thou hast strolled in the midst of stones of fire. Impeccable were you in your conduct from the day you were created, until wickedness was discovered in you. By your extensive trade you filled your innermost being with violence and sinned. Then I drove thee from the mountain of God, and the cherub that defended the entrance drove thee out from among the stones of fire. Your heart was haughty because of your

beauty. Thou didst nullify thy wisdom by the effect of thy splendour. I have cast you down to the earth; I have set you before kings to mock you." Ezekiel 28:13-17

According to Christian theology, the above passages from the Old Testament have a double meaning. Although these passages are primarily addressed to the King of Babylon (Isaiah) and to the King of Tyre (Ezekiel), it is clear from them that they are not addressed to either man. According to theologians, Satan (Lucifer) often acts through someone. In Genesis, he speaks through the serpent (about the serpent a little more below). In Isaiah he reigns through the king of Babylon, and in Ezekiel he captures the king of Tyre.

Another biblical passage, this time from the apocalypse of John describes the rebellion of the angels in this way:

"And there was a battle in heaven: Michael and his angels were to fight against the Dragon. And the Dragon and his angels came up to fight, but he did not prevail, and there was no more room for them in heaven. And the great Dragon was cast down, the Ancient Serpent, who is called the Devil and Satan, who deceived the whole inhabited earth, was cast down to the earth, and with him his angels were cast down". Revelation 12:7,9

Interestingly, Lucifer from the Isaiah passage, called Satan by Jesus, is here also called the Ancient Serpent.

The serpent, the perpetrator of the fall of the first humans already appears in the first book of the Bible, Genesis:

„And the serpent was more cunning than all the land animals which the Lord God had made. And he said to the woman, "Did God indeed say, Do not eat of the fruit of all the

trees of the garden?" The woman answered the serpent: "The fruit of the trees of this garden we may eat; only of the fruit of the tree which is in the midst of the garden, God said, You must not eat of it, nor even touch it, lest you die." Then said the serpent to the woman: "Surely you shall not die! But God knows that when you eat of the fruit of this tree, your eyes will be opened, and like God you will know good and evil". Genesis 3:1,5

Yahweh required blind faith from the beginning. The serpent argued that only knowledge would give understanding of the truth.

Satan, the Devil, the Dragon, the Ancient Serpent, Lucifer - some names are believed to have power.

The Bible contains the threat that one day every knee will bend at the sound of the terrible name Jesus. Probably fear is supposed to be the default state of mind of

believers. In view of this, it is perhaps surprising that it is the name Lucifer that causes a negative connotation in the beleaguered people. After all, no knee will bend at the name Lucifer, because this name has the power to raise from the knees.

The Christian saviour from reality, Jesus, also said this about Lucifer:

„I will no longer speak much with you, for the ruler of this world is coming. Yet he has nothing of his own in me". - John 14:30

Delusional believers who have trouble coming to terms with reality recognise that the one true natural world that exists for sure is ruled by Lucifer. The real world is therefore Luciferian. The delusional heavens, on the other hand, are a divine reality. Jesus saying: "Yet he has nothing of his own in me" as if to affirm that there is nothing real in himself.

But also a Christian could write interestingly about Lucifer. This is what St Ambrose of Milan wrote about him in the 4th century in a work entitled: "Carmen Auroraae".

Text translated from Latin into English by John A. McGuckin:

"The herald of the day now sounds, Watchful in the depth of night, Telling travellers that first light has come, Cutting off each night from night.
Thereby the Bringer of Light is roused, And frees the skies of darkness."

Lucifer frees the skies of darkness.

Satan or Lucifer are not real entities. So are God Yahweh, or any other god), as well as christ, angels and others. They are creations of the human mind, sometimes taking the form of delusions. Satan and Lucifer are seen

by Christian theology unequivocally as one and the same being, which for them is synonymous with the enemy of their delusional god; who was the first to lose faith in god. Ecclesia Luciferi proclaims the glory of a name that has become a symbol of godlessness.

Traditional Satanism

Satan Summoning His Legions - Thomas Lawrence (1797)

The term Satanism refers to and is closely related to the concept of Satan. Satan is a figure derived from the Yahwist tradition. The followers of Yahwism were the first to give the name Satan to one of the rebellious angels of the god Yahweh:

"And the great dragon, the ancient serpent, called the devil and Satan, deceiving the whole world, was cast down. He was cast down to the earth, and with him his angels were also cast down". Rev. 12:9

For the purposes of this chapter, I will use the reasoning used in the previous chapter as the issues are closely interlinked.

In the book of Isaiah in chapter 15, verses 12-15 it says:

"How is it that you fell from the heavens,
Shining One, Son of the Dawn?
How did you fall to the earth,
Thou who didst conquer the nations?
You who spoke in your heart:
I will ascend to the heavens;
Above the stars of God
I will set my throne.

I will sit down on the Mount of Sessions,
At the ends of the north.
I will ascend to the tops of the clouds,
I shall be like the Most High.
What do you mean? You have been cast down
to Sheol
To the very bottom of the Abyss!"

And this is how this text reads in Latin according to the Vulgate, the first translation of the Bible into Latin, which was written in the 4th century AD. The author of the translation was Saint Jerome.

*12 quomodo cecidisti de caelo **lucifer** qui mane oriebaris corruisti in terram qui vulnerabas gentes*
13 qui dicebas in corde tuo in caelum conscendam super astra Dei exaltabo solium meum sedebo in monte testamenti in lateribus aquilonis

The Latin translation of this passage uses the name Lucifer explicitly. Isaiah's text here parallels the words attributed to Jesus about Satan:

"Then he said to them: "I saw Satan, falling from heaven like lightning". - Luke 10:18

These texts demonstrate that Satan and Lucifer are seen as the same person.

Followers of the Nazarene prophet also gave Satan other proud names: Accuser, Ruler of this World, Ruler of the powers of the air, Enemy, Evil, Evil Spirit (for more on the origin of this name, see the chapter Angra Mainyu), Unclean Spirit, Ancient Serpent, Dragon, Ruler of Hellfire.

Of the many belief systems, magical or philosophical systems wishing to call themselves Satanism, for obvious reasons those that allude to the traditional Satan are closest to it. All other cults should not call themselves Satanism. These are non-Satanic belief systems, often in various ancient and pagan deities, or in other revealed (imaginary) supernatural entities.

There are also pathological organizations that seek out adepts from among people with psychopathic and sociopathic tendencies, or those who have such disorders, which teach that doing "bad things" is a sign of Satanism. Cynical leaders of such organizations or rather cults try to use their members, that is, their disturbed victims, for their criminal purposes. Such cults are not satanic. They are pathological and criminal. Satanism does not originate from mental disorders, it is the Abrahamic religions that originate from man with mental disorders.

The claim that true Satanism must be linked to belief in some theistic deity is false.

First of all, all deities that have ever existed and their names were invented by man and written down in various books that he himself declared sacred or cursed. These beings without man would not exist. Man without them, yes.

Secondly, Judeo-Christian theology, from which the enemy of the theistic God Yahweh, Satan originated argues that anyone who does not recognize the self-proclaimed son of God Jesus and denies that he is the messiah is acting under the influence of Satan:

"And every spirit,
who does not recognize Jesus is not of God;
and this is the spirit of Antichrist,
Who, as you have heard, is coming
and is already in the world." 1 John 4:3

"Who is a liar, if not he who denies that Jesus is the Christ? He is the antichrist who casts doubt on the Father and the Son." 1 John 2:22

"For many deceivers have gone out into the world who refuse to recognize that Jesus Christ came in the flesh. Such a one is a deceiver and antichrist." 2 John 1:7

And the greatest sin according to this philosophy is not believing in a god:

"...who go to perdition because they have not accepted the love of the truth in order to receive salvation. Therefore God allows deception to work on them, so that they will believe a lie, so that all who have not believed the truth (the gospel) but have taken a liking to iniquity will be judged." 2 Thess 2:10-12

These writings prove that the real core of Traditional Satanism is disbelief in the

self-proclaimed messiah Jesus and his teachings.

Therefore, a philosophy that does not recognize Jesus, that denies that Jesus is the Christ, questions the Father and the Son, and refuses to recognize that Jesus Christ came in the flesh is not of god, is Satanism. And it is not some contrived Satanism arising from drug-induced fantasies or speculations, but Satanism commanded from the religious writings of the Yahwism faction, from which the very name Satan derives.

Moreover, Satanism can and even should be seen as a worldview that not only rejects belief in the Judeo-Christian god but is the very absence of all belief in any theistic superstition, for the reason that this is the greatest possible sin according to all theistic religions.

Definitions

Satan and Satanism

Satan

Satan is the primordial rebellion against the tyranny and madness of a demented dictator. Satan is knowledge, Satan is sin because knowledge is sin, it is knowledge, it is the wisdom of this world, which this enemy of all that is human, this mad god of the Bronze Age hates with all his rotten heart. For if the first crime worthy of the punishment of eternal death consisted in knowing good and evil, in receiving knowledge, for if the wages of this sin is death, then man of flesh and blood, devoid of the divine fear of the Arch-human, will side with sin, imaginary crime and eternal death, will side with truth. Satan is a powerful symbol of the instinctive, natural to all free and therefore 'sinful' spirits,

opposition and rebellion against every form of dictatorship and tyranny, even that tyranny of false love enforced by fear of the wrath of the deity and eternal death.

Satanism.

Satanism is the path to the power of Will and inner 'sinful' freedom as opposed to the philosophy of subjugation and delusional guilt. Satanism is the truth about the often cruel and merciless nature of things as opposed to the lie of an imaginary afterlife.

Satanism is abundant life in the glory of flesh and blood, here and now instead of spiritual vegetation awaiting the 'great day of wrath' of an imaginary deity.

Satanism is the belief in a sole and sinless life before death. For original sin is a lie.

Antitheist

The property of the man-slave is the need to have a master over him. Whoever or whatever that master may be. It is a property of the man-slave.

The bird locked in a cage, ignorant of the world outside, not knowing what its wings are for. That broken under the master's whip, a little lost man, frightened at the thought of fighting the demons of the real world on his own, with the terrifying awareness of living here and now until death, which is the end. Death is the end of life - this is the truth revealed by the demon of knowledge.

The so-called spiritual man, a slave of delusion, who should rather be called a man without spirit, a man of frightened heart, who has not grown up to live in the body, the earth, who is still a lost puppy when there is no one around to show him the way, to protect him from the greatest danger for a

puppy - the truth of an indifferent, dark and cold universe, where the opposite of life - the dark vacuum - prevails. Such a man will seek a master, whoever or whatever that master may be. So long as the lord gives him illusory hope, comforts and protects him from the truth of the end of life. So long as there is something there, so long as he is not afraid.

Man, the puppy keeps looking back, even when he has seemingly grown in body, keeps looking back and thinking to himself - may someone protect me from this terrible truth that everyone really has to live alone until death, and there may be nothing there, just a cold eternity in the void. A man terrified by the truth about the nature of things will readily accept the hand of god or devil stretched out towards him, those deities or demons coming from his own mind, terribly tormented by reality. Such a man will willingly yield to the demons born of his own fears and submit to them like a slave to a

master, not knowing and not even wanting to know that he himself created these masters, out of fear. For there is nothing there. The hereafter is an invention, a speculation and a delusion. A god or devil born in the mind can become a master, but the strong man, the true man, this animal without fear, this Arch-human knows that it is he himself who creates such masters and can control them, but he can also kill them and become a god or devil for himself. He can be born again, but he can also die or depart into chaos and madness.

The theist is a man-slave, an ungrown puppy who may never grow up again. For the false god and the false Satan are jealous and deceitful gods, waging an eternal war for dominion over the mind of lost man. The reborn Arch-human, however, can become the true god or Satan, or kill both when he believes that he is the beginning and end of the imaginary universe.

For there is nothing there.

Praise the Lord

"I form the light, and create darkness: I make peace, and create evil: I the LORD do all these things" Isaiah 45.7

Evil is the god, madness is the god, cruelty is the god, pestilence, cancer, ulcers, war, rape. The insane monster and psychopath is he who, knowing all things, who, knowing what is to come, creates these games of death where fangs and claws and black plague rule. For his entertainment and pleasure he has created these contests to the death to relieve his eternal boredom. What more entertaining than watching a child die of cancer and the despair of its parents, what more rejoicing to a mind corrupted and deranged from eternal boredom than to admire the rape of a child by a priest of this

god. Is he not a reflection of his god? How comforting to the old degenerate must have been the spectacle of the torture and burning at the stake of countless innocent women. Is not the inquisitor an image of his god?

God is insane and corrupt to the marrow of his bones, god is contemptible, god is the enemy of man.

If one who believes in good and evil, he must recognise that god is not good. He must recognise the fact that Satan is the rebellion against the tyranny and madness of a demented dictator. Satan is knowledge, Satan is sin because knowledge is sin, it is knowledge, it is the wisdom of this world, which this enemy of all that is human, this mad god of the Bronze Age hates with all his rotten heart.

Natural Born Satanist
Satanism according to the Ecclesia Luciferi

Franciszek Zmurko - Morning Star

The satanic philosophy of Ecclesia Luciferi preaches an egoistic individualism, which attaches the greatest importance to one's own benefit and that of one's offspring.

The Satanism it preaches implies a total belief only in oneself, hostility to any form of belief in a 'higher power' or in imaginary supernatural entities, reliance on oneself and bearing all the consequences of one's own

decisions and choices, and an understanding of the choice to end one's conscious life in suffering.

The Satanism of Ecclesia Luciferi is an individualistic elitism that recognises that what distinguishes members of the elite from the rest of society is the desire to establish oneself as a distinct and unique individual. Such an individual establishes patterns of behaviour for himself or herself, rather than adopting them from the crowd, considered secondary and mindless.

Equality has never existed, does not exist and will not exist. Egalitarianism is a utopia.

Ecclesia Luciferi states that a person's unwillingness to

self-perfection, psycho-physical development, exploration of the inner and the outer, to attempt to achieve subjective perfection or self-elevation in order to lead and show the way to others, means self-debasement of such an individual and places such an

individual in a subordinate position to the Satanist. On the other hand, any individual who consciously tries to parasitise others, commits crimes against property and life, decides himself to be definitively and irreversibly cut off from society.

The law of talion, that is, the commensurability of the sanction with the gravity of the crime committed, must be applied to such an individual.

Ecclesia Luciferi preaches and exhorts to live in accordance with the eternal and immutable laws governing the inert universe. The Luciferian natural order of things is morally indifferent, there is no good or evil in it. It is governed by the godless selfishness of nature, which makes the development and survival of the species possible.

A paradise in which death and suffering will no longer exist is an illusion of the weak or manipulated. True eternity is endless darkness.

And although life itself may be immortal until it disappears as mysteriously as it appeared and is passed on through genes to the next generation, a single individual lives in his consciousness only for a relatively short time and only for this time can he decide about his life and death. And if in this finite time he does not pass on his genes inherited from previous generations to his offspring, his lifeline will expire forever. The eternity of his life will continue as long as his genes are passed on to the next generation in this Luciferian order of things, in this peculiar godless reincarnation of successive totally godless beings, untainted in their instinctive nature by religious illusions, in an ever-repeating cycle of life and death in this Luciferian eternal circle of life.

Satanist according to Ecclesia Luciferi

I identify with all that Satan represents in his very essence, and what the worshippers of superstition call sin.

I identify with everything that the worshippers of imaginary gods hate the most, and of which Satan, whom they have called the master of this world, is for them a symbol. I am characterised by innate disbelief, natural instincts dating back to the ancient godless times of beastliness, earthly carnality, sinful self-determination, truly Luciferian pride, the inherent egoism of all mortal beings, the morality of an indifferent universe and inherited mortality. I have an inherent satanic contempt for the mental simplicity of the worshippers of a Bronze Age desert deity and for the contrary to nature divine laws derived from yahwist worship.

I will not chop off my leg, I will not cut off my hand, I will not pluck out my eye because there is no fear in me of the burning love of a false messiah. For myself I am the way, the truth and the life.

Are you also a Satanist?

According to Christian theology, anyone who does not believe in the insane philosophy of imaginary and blameless crime and eternal punishment for it in the hereafter is a Satanist. Everyone, without exception. For Christians there is no middle ground. Either you are a slave to their messiah Jesus or you are a follower of Satan. Here is an example from their "holy books". To begin with the words of the "saviour":

"He who is not with me is against me; and he who does not gather with me scatters". Lk 11.23

Further developing this thought, here is what awaits those who do not believe the one "truth":

"...who go to perdition because they have not accepted the love of the truth (the gospel) in order to receive salvation.
Therefore God allows deception to work on them, so that they will believe a lie, so that all who have not believed the truth (the gospel) but have taken a liking to iniquity will be judged." 2 Thess 2:10-12

There is a clear threat here against all those who reject blind faith in 'revealed truth' unsupported by any evidence, and what is more, the author implies that the rejection of sacred speculations incompatible with logic and with the real picture of reality occurs as a result of their deity allowing deception to operate on doubters.
Oh how twisted and deceitful is the philosophy of this anti-human sect.

Continuing with the "good news":

"...And the same word has now secured the heavens and the earth as being preserved for the fire for the day of judgment and perdition of ungodly men." - 2 P 3:7

Fire thus awaits unbelievers in God (the ungodly).

*"If anyone is not found written in the book of life,
he was cast into the lake of fire". Rev 20.15*

*"And the devil, who deceives them,
was cast into the lake of fire and sulphur,
Where the Beast and the False Prophet are.
And they shall suffer torment day and night
for ever and ever". - Rev 20.10*

So, without any understatement, the unbelievers will end up in the fire just like their master the Devil.

It is clear from the above texts that, according to Christians, if you do not believe in their "good news" then you are professing Satanism and for that you will face eternal fire. There is no other alternative.

So perhaps, scornfully dismissing the fear of this, created in the sick minds of the preachers of the 'good news', threat of death by fire at the hands of the 'prince of peace and love' on doomsday, it is best to simply embrace your natural Satanism?

And another interesting quote at the end:

"when you await and seek to hasten the coming of the day of God, which will cause the lit heavens to go to destruction and the stars to be scattered in fire". - 2P 3.12

Christians expect and even seek to hasten the doom in the fire. How nice. I wonder what would happen if religious fanatics took control of nuclear weapons?

The reality is the Antichrist

There is probably nowhere more emphatically and convincingly demonstrated what Christianity really is than in the letters of the wandering, self-proclaimed prophet Paul.

It is a manifestation of how this philosophy of the hereafter is hostile to what is true, natural, human - animal, instinctive. And here is an example of this madness taken from the letter to the Romans:

"For we know that the Law is spiritual. And I am carnal, sold into slavery to sin. For I do not understand what I do, because I do not do what I want, but what I hate - that is what I

do. If, on the other hand, I do what I do not want, I thereby admit the Law to be good. Therefore, it is no longer I who do it, but sin dwelling in me.

For I am aware that in me, that is, in my flesh, the good does not dwell; for it is easy for me to want what is good, but to perform it I do not. For I do not do the good that I want, but I do the evil that I do not want. And if I do what I do not want, it is no longer I who do it, but sin that dwells in me. So I find in myself this law, that when I want to do good, evil is imposed upon me. For the inner man is pleased with the Law of God. In my members, however, I perceive another law, which fights against the law of my mind and brings me into slavery under the law of sin dwelling in my members. O wretched man that I am! Who shall deliver me from the body, [which leads to] this death? Thanks be to God through Jesus Christ our Lord! Thus with the

mind I serve the law of God, but with the flesh the law of sin". - Rom 7. 14-25

This is a wonderful description of the inner struggle between delusion and reality, with one's own body and with nature. Such a struggle necessarily leads sooner rather than later to madness.

The author of the Letter to the Romans is clearly suffering, fighting against the natural instincts and needs of the flesh, which he considers sinful.

He also believes that there are two persons living inside him. This imaginary 'inner man', the one who wants to follow a made-up 'law of God' is the good one. Whereas the other one, the one who wants to act according to the natural, instinctive needs of the body and mind wants to sell him into slavery to 'sin'. Perhaps Paul was also ultimately close to suicide. This may be evidenced by his desperate cry for help at the end of this

lengthy speech: "Wretched am I man! Who will deliver me from the flesh [which leads towards] this death? "

Fortunately, a saviour, whom Paul had met in a vision in the desert, comes to his aid. He had never seen him in his supposed earthly shell. The saviour appeared to him in his mind in a vision. And this saviour liberates Paul from this bodily suffering. He liberates him from reality. From the only body Paul ever had. According to Paul's delusions, the saviour liberates him from the only life that exists for sure. Life in the body, here and now. He liberates him from the natural needs of the body, from the natural instincts. I am not an expert in psychiatry, but is Christianity and other similar religions very far from psychiatric illnesses such as, for example, Bipolar Affective Disorder (BPAD)?

Here is a brief overview of Bipolar Affective Disorder:

Bipolar Affective Disorder (BPAD) is manifested by alternating episodes of depression and mania, separated by periods of remission. The frequency of relapses and exacerbations varies from patient to patient - if the number of relapses and exacerbations exceeds four per year, we speak of rapid cycling affective disorder.

In many patients, depressive symptoms occur more frequently and last longer. In the case of mania, there is an elevated mood, racing thoughts, hallucinations, irritability and even a tendency to aggression. In milder variants of the illness, we are dealing with hypomania, with a milder course, without manufacturing symptoms
(e.g. hallucinations).

What is certain is that in Paul's case there is an attempt to suppress reality and to follow a voice binding him to paradise.

In summary, hallucinations, denial of reality and blind faith are the way to salvation (certainly salvation from reality in the first place), while the instinctive, natural needs of the body and mind, the very carnality hated by Christians, is a selling into slavery to sin. Simply put, nature is the Antichrist, and carnal man is the Satanist.

But how could it be otherwise. After all, the origin of all three Yahwistic religions was given by Abraham, who, after hearing voices in his head, decided to sacrifice his son. Yahwism is falsehood and delusion. Satanism is a rebellion against this madness.

The Real Satanic Bible

Over the centuries, many great books on witchcraft, alchemy, magic and the occult have been written. Many of them found their way into the Church's index of forbidden books. Some were even attributed to the co-authorship of the Devil himself. However, there is one exceptional book that has proven to have real ungodly power. First, however, it is necessary to provide a historical context to help understand how

revolutionary and ungodly theses were contained in this book.

A certain Anglican bishop by the name of James Ussher (1581-1656), calculated on the basis of a chronology based on the 'infallible word of God' that the Earth was created on 22 October 4004 BC, a Saturday, at six o'clock in the evening.

As is well known, this is an undeniable truth revealed to the author of a book called Genesis by one of the desert deities called Yahweh.

In this book, it is revealed that the entire universe was created some 6,000 years ago, in six working days from nothing, and that on the seventh day Yahweh had to rest.

The book also reveals to us the secret of the creation of the first man, who was created from sand, and his woman, created from his rib while he slept. This woman later committed the most terrible crime in the universe - at the instigation of a talking snake,

she ate fruit from one of the magic trees in the garden. And there were many magic trees there, each with a different power. And it was as a result of this act that earthquakes, hurricanes, fires, floods, tsunamis occurred, death and disease came into the world and all creatures were doomed to die and suffer. Never mind that it was a woman who ate the fruit. From then on, throughout the ages, innocent bunnies and kittens and even pregnant deer would suffer and die in pain because Yahweh had cursed the woman.

A certain turning point was to occur when the god Yahweh because a few centuries, by means of a spirit impregnated a Jewish virgin who gave birth to his son so that this son could be sacrificed to this Yahweh and killed for three days. As a result of this landmark event, anyone who believes this will be saved from the consequences of the crime of the woman from the magic garden.

For centuries, this was an undeniable truth. Then, in the year 1859, the English naturalist, geologist and traveller Charles Darwin published a book entitled: "On the Origin of Species". This book described the entirely natural process of the creation of new species without the involvement of a god or other supernatural forces. God was simply no longer needed to describe reality. It turned out that reality was best and most accurately described by the completely natural processes of nature and the completely natural laws of nature and physics.

Darwin even included some 'prophecies' in his book that came true. Such as the 'prophecy' that there must be so-called intermediate forms between different animal species in the fossil record. Thus, in 1861, two years after the publication of 'On the Origin of Species', a fossil of an 'intermediate form' between reptiles and birds was discovered in Germany and named

Archaeopteryx. In another 'shocking' book published in 1871: "The Descent of Man", Darwin stated that man, the one who, according to the book of Genesis, was to subjugate the whole earth and all animals, was descended from an ape-like animal and his remains would be found in Africa. This is what happened. In 1924, the remains of an 'ape' were discovered in a cave in South Africa and named Australopithecus. It turned out that the 'ape' walked upright, on two legs, and was something 'intermediate' between humans and other apes.

This was another of Darwin's 'prophecies' that came true. Today, the scientific world has thousands of fossils preserved or literally carved in stone (as opposed to mythical stone tablets with commandments engraved with the finger of a god, which no one has ever seen), proving that 'that devil's' theory of evolution is true, that this walking 'holiness' of man is descended from animals

and is nothing more than one species of animal. This devil Darwin's book caused shock and holy indignation among the lunatics believing blindly in the "sacred, revealed books". Darwin was considered a disciple of the devil who wrote under the inspiration of Satan to destroy the only sacred revealed truth.

Considering what a revolution in the world of biology and religion and in the mentality of people the book "On the Origin of Species" has caused, how many "good" Christians it has killed faith in, and that it is still destroying religious myths and dogmas, it is safe to call it Satan's Bible. That true Satanic Bible, possessing a truly diabolical power to destroy blind faith and superstition. The work 'On the Origin of Species' is undoubtedly one of the most important books in the history of science. But as we know, science as an enemy of faith is also satanic.

Biblia Satanae

Biblia Satanae is a collection of godless and heretical religious writings, having different forms but characterised by a common message. Biblia Satanae, unlike the claims of divine inspiration of the Judeo-Christian Bible, is the Word of Man. It is not revealed or inspired by any deity. The godless Satanism that is a common feature of all its writings stems from a rejection of the concept of blind faith consistent with its definition in the writings of the Nazarene sect as: "the certainty of what is expected, the

conviction of what is not seen", and the pursuit of knowledge that leads to Satanic awakening or enlightenment.

Biblia Satanae consists of six books:

- Genesis Secundum Serpentem
- Antichristus
- Angelus Satanae - Encyclica
- Epistle to the Damned
- Epistle to the Ungodly
- Pseudoapocalypsis

Here is a brief introduction to these books:

Genesis Secundum Serpentem.

The title Genesis Secundum Serpentem can be translated as The Beginning According to the Serpent. The first book of the Hebrew Torah is called Bereshit, which means In the Beginning in Hebrew. The word Torah itself

originally means instruction or warning. The title Genesis Secundum Serpentem should therefore be read as a warning of the Serpent of what may come if one gives credence to religious delusions at the beginning. Genesis Secundum Serpentem points first and foremost to the irrationality, insanity and cruelty of primitive laws invented by superstitious people and whose origin was attributed to imaginary gods. It is a look at the old myths as if through the eye of the Ancient Serpent, who convinced the mythical first men that if they defied the illogical divine laws, they would gain forbidden knowledge. In the beginning there was blind faith, from which was born yahwistic (and more broadly theistic) madness, a virus that infected human brains, that caused the man infected with it to choose irrationality and delusion over reason and knowledge. This virus was able to drive the followers of an invented god to torture

and burn heretics and witches at the stake, because the smell of burnt flesh was pleasing to the lord from the start.

Slavery, genocide, intolerance, murdering dissenters, treating women like cattle, stoning homosexuals.... these are all precepts of the law which, according to blindly believing fanatics, was supposed to come directly from the god Yahweh. Bereshit means In the beginning. In the beginning was faith, then came intolerance and violence.

Antichristus

Antichristus is an anti-theistic, Luciferian synoptic apocrypha. It is characterised by a considerable similarity of relationship to the biblical gospels. It is therefore essentially a synoptic book with the gospels. The book is distinguished, however, by its own different and completely ungodly theological

conception. Since Antichristus is a book devoid of any divine inspiration, it can therefore be considered an apocrypha.

Antichristus is a Luciferian heretical gospel according to the Christian definition of heresy as an interpretation of the claims of the Christian faith, consisting in isolating an issue and presenting it in a way that opposes the whole teaching of the faith.

Antichristus rejects the Christian deposit of faith in its entirety.

The book calls for a complete rejection of primitive and naïve religious belief and a search for self-enlightenment through godless knowledge (gnosis).

Angelus Satanae Encyclica

Angelus Satanae - Encyclica is a heretical apocrypha taking the form of an encyclical. According to the statement in 2 Corinthians 11:14 "And no wonder, for Satan himself

assumes the form of an angel of light". - the content of the encyclical is deliberately synoptic with the oldest writings of the Nazarene sect, but with a completely opposite theological concept. The topics dealt with in Angelus Satanae relate to doctrinal and organisational matters of the model Satanic Church and are of a general nature.

Letters

Other letters: Epistle to the Damned and Epistle to the Ungodly were written in a similar manner to the Encyclical using the method of the Mystery of the Godlessness (for an exposition of the teachings of the Satanic System of Disbelief Ecclesia Luciferi, see the book The Satanic Kerygma).

Pseudoapocalypsis

Apocalypsis, from the Greek ἀποκάλυψις apokalypsis means to unveil, or remove the veil. Pseudo-apocalypsis is a false apocalypse. While the Christian book of revelation claims to present the truth about the end of the temporal system of things and the following eternity in the hereafter, knowledge obtained by revelation (delusion), the Pseudoapocalypsis being a fiction unveils the veil of hell of religious delusions standing on the threshold of mental disorder or sometimes, as in the case of the Apocalypse, exceeding this threshold.

The heretical books comprising the Biblia Satanae form a truly Satanic Bible.

Ecclesia Luciferi

*"To all who have not this doctrine, to those who,
they say, have not known the depths of Satan"
Rev 2:24*

The term Ecclesia comes from the Greek
(ἐκκλησία ekklēsía) and means assembly.
The Ecclesia Luciferi is a spiritual immaterial
Luciferian assembly or convocation to which
anyone can belong at will by virtue of
understanding and acknowledging its
ambiguous teachings as their own.

Ecclesia Luciferi can best be described as a spiritual satanic sect. It is a spiritual entity arbitrarily emerging from a satanic system of unbelief.

The definition of a sect should be taken as that which states that the sect contests, in contrast to the institutionalised church, a particular social order and pursues its own religious and ethical ideals, and that the way to perfect itself is not through sacraments but through personal experience.

Man is a herd animal, which is why it is important for many, including Satanists of various kinds, to belong to an organisation, a group, a church. People of different religions and denominations, including satanists, often define the church mainly or exclusively by their active participation in the structures. And while this human need to be part of a flock of some kind is understandable, the Ecclesia Luciferi symbolises an egoistic individualism that places the greatest

importance on self-interest and reliance on the self, and an individualistic elitism, which recognises that what distinguishes members of the elite from the rest of society is the desire to establish oneself as a distinct and unique individual. Such an individual sets patterns of behaviour for himself or herself, rather than adopting them from the crowd, which is considered secondary and mindless.

All the writings of the Ecclesia Luciferi, those which form the basic collection of books entitled the Traditional Satanic Bible contain a satanic, strongly individualistic philosophy, which is the complete opposite of the Judeo-Christian philosophy of divesting oneself of natural human instincts and carnal needs, of guilt for being born as a human being in flesh and blood to the only true life here and now. The satanic philosophy of Ecclesia Luciferi is a rejection of any baseless belief in life after life, a renunciation of belief in a heavenly reward

for slavish obedience to the dictatorship of a god (e.g. Yahweh) or a second death in eternal fire for lack of blind obedience.

The basic tenets of the philosophy of the Satanic System of Disbelief, Ecclesia Luciferi, known as the mystery of godlessness, are contained in the Articles of Disbelief.

Non Credo in Deum

I reject the unfounded belief in a god, another of the many dead gods, Father of all impotence,
Creator of an delusional heaven and enemy of the earth, the opposite of the visible things and equal to the invisible ones.
I reject the belief in a human son of the invisible god, who is born of human fantasies.
God from Man,

Madness from Madness,
God delusional from the real man.
Created, not born,
Co-substantial with the human Father,
and through Him many evils have happened.
It was through man's ignorance and for his enslavement that He descended from a non-existent heaven.
And according to the delusion He accepted the sacrifice of a human virgin and became a false demigod.
He was hanged according to the law for blasphemy, but was not buried.
And superstition arose on the third day,
And he reached the very unconscience; he sits there at the right hand of the Father of all impotence.
And he shall return again and again to judge, not the truly living, but those already dead to the flesh,
and there will be no end to the kingdom of superstition.

I reject belief in the spirit of bondage, the lord of delusion and the false accuser, who, like a god, comes from man.

Who, with the delusional god and his self-proclaimed son, jointly receive the praise and glory belonging only to him who truly, in his madness, is the creator of the gods; who truly inspired the false prophets.

I reject belief in hypocritical churches.

I confess the Self-Remission of sins.

And I look forward to an eternity among the dead and life abundant here and now.

Amen.

Ten Ungodly Words

1. Let the absence of faith in the gods be your certainty.

Not belief in their non-existence, but lack of faith.

Let Satan be your certainty.

He lacks faith in God.

2. Let the certainty of the absence of inherited guilt never leave thee. Remember thou art innocent. The Saviour is needed by sinners.

3. May contempt for God's plan of salvation be ever strong in thee. Let the false deity sacrifice his own children. You have nothing to do with it.

4. You don't need a calling to become a priest of Satan. You are one by virtue of unbelief. For unbelievers shall not inherit the kingdom of heaven.

5. Let the churches be alien to you. Let your body become the temple of Satan.

6. Let unbelief and scepticism be your strength. Faith is the enemy of certainty. Certainty gives real power. Faith is feigned certainty.

7. All sacred books are the word of God. All books were written by man. Man is god.

8. Let faith in revelations fill you with revulsion.

It is because of this madness that millions have already lost their lives. Many more will lose.

9. Do not let yourself be deceived by God-fearing people who preach tolerance and freedom of religion. There will be no tolerance for you. It will only be for people like them, followers of delusions.

They will hate you for your instinctive, satanic certainty that the gods are false.

10: Satan, the only real one.

Look in the mirror.

The basic books of the Ecclesia Luciferi are the books included in the Traditional Satanic Bible collection: Biblia Satanae, The Satanic Kerygma and Missale Satanae.

Biblia Satanae is the primary book using the method of doubt - the mystery of godlessness.

It is a tool for anti-theistic disenchantment. An understanding of the method used in it and the message of this book can be applied with equal force to any 'revealed' book, not just the Judeo-Christian Bible.

The mystery of godlessness is an anti-divine and therefore satanic power to oppose the gods.

The Satanic Kerygma contains a godless, satanic doctrine, a theology of godlessness - the biblical mystery of godlessness.

It constitutes a study of theistic delusional truths and the path of man's transformation to a state of total godlessness. If we take the Latin maxim: fides quaerens intellectum - faith seeking understanding - as a definition of theology, then a theology of godlessness means an understanding that rejects theistic faith altogether. This peculiar understanding and rejection of belief in imaginary gods leads to what the book calls instinctive Satanism.

The book The Satanic Kerygma is, for the most part, written in the form of a parabola and its teachings are allegorical in nature.

The book Missale Satanae contains a description of satanic rites such as the satanic mass and exorcism. Although these rites can indeed be performed, the main idea is to reflect spiritually on their meaning and to stimulate the dark imagination.

The Traditional Satanic Bible also includes, among other things, evil spirit-inspired letters addressed to all those individuals who have the whim and will to participate in the spiritual sect Ecclesia Luciferi.

Finally, it is worth recalling the words of Friedrich Nietzche, which perfectly represent the attitude of the Satanic individual:

"What do I care about the rest? - The rest is only humanity. - One must be superior to

humanity by strength, by heights of spirit, - by contempt...".

Anyone and everyone can belong to Ecclesia Luciferi.

The next part of the book, the next few chapters will be dedicated to the subject of magic, demon summoning and demonic possession.

Satanic Magic

To make yourself invisible

Acquire seven black beans. Start the whole rite on Wednesday, before sunrise. Take the head of a dead man and place one bean in its mouth, two in the cavity of the nose, two in the eye sockets, two in the ears, on the head make the character you find in the engraving. And when you have done everything bury the head so that the face faces upwards.

For nine days, before sunrise, water it every morning using the best brandy. On the eighth day you will find the said spirit asking you the question, "What is withering here?" You, in turn, will answer: "I am watering my plant." Then the spirit will say: "Give me the bottle, I wish to water it myself." In response you must refuse him, even if he repeats the request. Then he will extend his hand and show you the same figure you have drawn on your head. Then you can be sure that you are dealing with the right spirit, the spirit of the head. This is because there is a danger that some other spirit might try to deceive you, which would have bad consequences, in which case your operation would certainly fail.

Only then can you give him the bottle, and he will water his head and leave. The next day, which is the ninth, when you return, you will see that the beans have germinated. Take the sprout and place it in your mouth

and look at your reflection in the mirror, if you don't see anything it is good, in the same way you can try the others, you can place them either in your mouth or in the child's mouth. Those seeds that don't produce the invisibility effect should be buried with your head.

How to make a girl dance naked

Write on virgin parchment the first character from the figure shown here, do it with the blood of a bat. Later, place it on the blessed stone over which the Mass was recited. After this, whenever you wish to use it, place it under the threshold, or under the door through which she will have to pass. And when she passes through, then she will go into a strange frenzy, she will undress and become completely naked. And when she begins to dance, if no one pulls this sign, she will dance until she dies, her face will be

twisted and her body will twist, arousing more compassion and pity than desire.

The grotesque magical rituals presented above are taken from the work entitled: "Grimorium Verum", supposedly written in 1517, but actually written most likely in the mid-18th century.

What is magic?

White magic, black magic, satanic magic, magic... It is, in general, a body of beliefs and practices based on the belief in the existence of supernatural forces that can be controlled by means of appropriate spells and specific actions.

The above rituals are an example of how ridiculous, grotesque and idiotic a belief in supernatural reality and supernatural powers can take form.

However, I do not deny that there is 'magic' which holds that the subconscious is responsible for magical actions and can be programmed to achieve the desired changes. This programming takes place through the use of symbols and autosuggestion in a state of mind which, for example, Buddhists call samadhi and the chaots call gnosis.

Christians, such as Pentecostals, for example, can, with the right techniques and a strong belief in supernatural reality, put themselves into a state resembling collective hysteria, during which they may mumble something in unintelligible languages or even experience hallucinations.

If hallucinations, hysteria, fainting spells and meaningless babbling are to be called magic, then such 'magic' does indeed exist. Nevertheless, the human mind, still mysterious, with its subconscious, with its not fully understood phenomenon of self-awareness, can hide whole magical

worlds, sometimes manifested in dark dreams. It is there that still undiscovered and unrecognised, dark, fiendishly beautiful and blasphemous powers are hidden. They may become accessible to some people determined enough to dare to look there.

And here I would like to present some visualisation techniques that may be responsible for phenomena such as visions or appearances of phantoms. But first I will present a more scientific understanding of these phenomena.

Summoning Demons
Satanic Mysticism

Faust and the demon Mephistopheles

Followers of a belief in a personal Satan and in beings supposedly coming from another dimension or from another world, called demons, that is, so-called traditional Satanists or theistic Satanists sometimes claim to be able to summon these beings and to communicate with them, and sometimes,

for the most worthy, they even manage to talk to Satan himself in person.

Followers of other religions also sometimes claim to have managed to communicate with angels, Jesus, or that they have received a vision of the Virgin Mary, or hear the voice of a god in their heads.

From the beginning, our prehistoric, "pre-scientific" ancestors had to deal with existential problems, with survival, with adaptation, with powerful natural phenomena that were incomprehensible to them, with birth and death, with grief and with stress. So they created myths and beliefs to explain the origin of everything to them, they created a belief in life after death to stop being afraid of it. People sometimes experienced visions, voices in their head and strong emotions that seemed to come from somewhere beyond them. So they created ceremonies and rituals to help them contact the gods and the afterlife, called up shamans,

priests and prophets to guide and comfort them spiritually in this life, and finally to guide them to the other side, where "death and suffering will be no more".

With the development of science and technological advances, man began to take an interest in the structure of the human brain and its functions, including those related to religion. The field of knowledge known as the neuroscience of religion was born.

By studying the areas of the human brain responsible for the emotions and sensations of religious experiences, meditations, visions, voices in the head, etc., it was discovered that the human brain is responsible for religious experiences.

Among other things, it was discovered that:

„Our response to religious words is mediated at the juncture of three lobes (parietal, frontal, and temporal) and governs reaction

to language. The "voice of God" probably emanates from electrical activity in the temporal lobes, which are important to speech perception. Inner speech is interpreted as originating outside the self, when Broca's area switches on. Stress can influence our ability to determine origin of a voice. It is part of our fight-flight response, which can mobilize even when we try to relax. Unstressing phenomena can range from panic reactions, heaving sighs, excessive heat to shivers and bristling of the skin, throat constriction, watery eyes, light flashes or waves before the eyes, sudden muscular contractions, tingling sensations, and electric shocks. The right anterior cingulate turns on whether a stimulus originates in the environment or is an auditory hallucination. A wide variety of mystical sounds have been described ranging from the buzzing of bees, to the sounds of bells, stringed instruments, thunder, distant echoes, ocean waves, wind,

and muffled talk in unknown languages. The ability to construct internal representations of sensory stimuli underlies perception and cognition. Viewed objectively, these mindscapes are perfectly concrete manifestations but also have a subjective aspect when we become aware of them. Our consciousness is experienced through our perceptions. Any individual perception of the universe can occur as an internal or external experience. We may experience varying forms of an I-Thou dialogue along the continuum of extremely hyper- or hypo-arousal states. Sacred images are generated in the lower temporal lobe, which also responds to ritualistic use of imagery and iconography. Empathy needs a face. Fear and awesomeness originate in the amygdala. Religious emotions originate in the middle temporal lobe, generating bliss, awe, joy and

other feelings of well-being, as well as a sense of Presence".[1]

In my book The Satanic Kerygma, this is how I described 'interactions with demons' according to the Ecclesia Luciferi system:

The Visible and the Invisible

---

[1] How the Brain Creates the Feeling of God: The Emergent Science of Neurotheology - Iona Miller

Images of Demons

Reality of Demons - Extra-corporeal Reality

Immaterial, non-corporeal beings are real like dreams. They belong to the domain of the inner worlds.

Who are the images of demons?

Demons are creations of the Satanic Self-consciousness. By what appearances they make they may be called spirits, but in view of their task they are demons. Demons are servants and emissaries of Satanic Being. Because always subordinated to the purpose of deception, they are the executors of His orders. Demons, beings from the inner darkness, can take over the reason and will of those who are weak or untrained in controlling them: they can become as present as if they were real. As a result of the error or recklessness of the visualiser, they can, with their sinful perfection, rise above

human will and reason. They have the power to compel the performance of dark and terrible things. Including ultimate things. Lucifer is the centre of the inner demonic circle. Images of demons belong to Him, because He has the greatest power to compel the subconscious to create any sinful entity.

Even more so, they belong to Him because He has made them emissaries of His plan of deception to those who call upon them.

The images of the demons are present from the moment they are projected and throughout the hallucination.

Demons of the Ecclesia Luciferi Sect

The entire satanic system of disbelief, Ecclesia Luciferi can use the mystery and power of the knowledge of the extra-corporeal nature of demon images to deceive.

The teaching of doubt can appeal to Satanic Self-consciousness creating sinful entities at

will. However, one must always be aware of the danger of losing control and even the senses".

The Satanic System, Ecclesia Luciferi is consistent with the scientific description of reality and at the same time corresponds to the human need to experience spirituality. It is a spirituality that emerges from the natural "sinful" world, the rulership of which has been assigned to Satan.

It is not my intention to deny that man is able to experience visions during which it seems to him that he is communicating with someone else, with someone not of this world or dimension. A trained shaman or mystic is sometimes even able to bring himself to a state close to experiencing death by means of equivalent techniques.

"When the senses and mind cease to function actively, the body becomes like a corpse. The

death of the ego mirrors the process of a near-death experience (NDE)."[2]

Man for some reason has always needed to experience mystical experiences, he needed religion. But today, religion should no longer be based on ignorance. It is possible to successfully combine a realistic, scientific view of reality with the human need for spirituality.

The satanic system of disbelief in the reality of imaginary entities, Ecclesia Luciferi, describes a godless spirituality derived from sinful carnality.

---

[2] How the Brain Creates the Feeling of God: The Emergent Science of Neurotheology - Iona Miller

The Magus
Lucifer Rising

The Magician (I), from the Rider–Waite tarot deck

In the previous chapter, I addressed the issue of demon summoning from a more scientific angle, trying to explain what psycho-physical factors are behind the appearance of various phenomena such as visions or phantoms

appearing. That text was rather technical. This time I would like to present the more esoteric side of these phenomena, which I wrote about in my book The Satanic Kerygma, and which also belong to the Ecclesia Luciferi system. Although they are not the most relevant from the point of view of the philosophy of the system (The Mystery of Godlessness), this 'religious' dimension of the system may seem interesting to some.

Understanding these phenomena in an esoteric way and some of the techniques presented here are not my fantasies, nor are they invented by me. These are issues and techniques that have been known for hundreds of years. Their effectiveness has been proven. I have decided that there is no need to reinvent the wheel. Only the terminology, the names and the approach to some of the issues are slightly different. This is, of course, only an introduction or outline

of the subject. The subject is so rich and broad that a whole separate book could be written about it.

Excerpted from the book The Satanic Kerygma:

The Visible and the Invisible
Images of Demons
Reality of Demons - Extra-corporeal Reality

Immaterial, non-corporeal beings are real like dreams. They belong to the domain of the inner worlds. Who are the images of demons? Demons are creations of Satanic Self-consciousness. By what appearances they make they may be called spirits, but in view of their task they are demons. Demons are servants and emissaries of Satanic Being. Because always subordinated to the purpose of deception, they are the executors of His orders.

Demons, beings from the inner darkness, can take over the reason and will of those who are weak or untrained in controlling them: they can become as present as if they were real. As a result of the error or recklessness of the visualiser, they can, with their sinful perfection, rise above human will and reason. They have the power to compel the performance of dark and terrible things. Including ultimate things.

Lucifer is the centre of the inner demonic circle. Images of demons belong to Him, because He has the greatest power to compel the subconscious to create any sinful entity.

Even more so, they belong to Him because He has made them emissaries of His plan of deception to those who call upon them.

The images of the demons are present from the moment they are projected and throughout the hallucination.

This text is primarily concerned with one way of achieving a state of Satanic Self-Awareness. This is a state similar to that known, for example, in Esoteric Buddhism as Luminosity. This state can be achieved through various practices and techniques. One such method is to consciously enter a state of deep dreaming, and if the practitioner is able to remain conscious during this deep dreaming, he or she will be able to recognise the so-called luminosity of death and ultimately achieve the state of the Enlightened One.

Special meditation methods, such as sleep yoga, are used to achieve the state of lucid dreaming, but hallucinogenic plants such as the Bard's Sage or meditation recordings, recordings of so-called binural sounds, can also be helpful. Devices that send out light or sound signals are also used. However, meditative methods are the most advisable.

In a study published by Julian Mutz and Amir-Homayoun Javadi in Neuroscience of Consciousness in 2017, the authors showed that people who practise meditation for a longer period of time have more lucid dreams.

The aforementioned techniques aim to achieve a hybrid state of consciousness having the characteristics of both the real world and a dream, during which it would be advisable to try to transform this newly created reality. Once a person has learned to experience such a state, he or she can begin to practice visualising oneself as a deity - Lucifer - the Luminous. Transforming one's own identity into that of the divine.

By practising meditation on reality as dream-like, and the methods described above, such visualisation can be perceived as no less real than everyday reality.

This transformation of identity into a completely godless entity can also be seen as

a kind of possession. Its course and effects are described in my book The Satanic Kerygma as follows:

"With a kind of possession, man in unconsciousness turns to the Sinful Being as if to a dark god and communes with him in order to invite him into communion with himself and receive him into it. The response to this is the gift of doubt. During doubt, man surrenders his reason and his will completely to the Being. With his whole corporeal being, man expresses the acquiescence of the Anti-God. The system of unbelief calls man's response to the Anti-God manifested in him a possession".

Because according to The Satanic Kerygma:

"Lucifer is the centre of the inner demonic circle. The images of demons belong to him, because he has the greatest power to compel the subconscious to create every sinful entity".

It is up to the practitioner to be able to create images of demons.

These demons are visualisations of emotions commonly considered 'negative'. According to a tantric practice called transformation theory, these 'negative' emotions such as lust, hatred, greed, pride are used as part of the path. As necessary elements on the path to true liberation.

These things that people think are bad, visualised, serve my will. I control them and can transform them at will. I will use them to achieve the goal, perfect indifference. True enlightenment involves transcending attachment to dual categories such as pure and impure, permitted and forbidden (good and bad).

As the Guhyasamaja Tantra states, 'the sage who makes no distinction attains the state of the Awakened One'.

If the practitioner has the will to attribute some demon names to these emotions or the signs corresponding to these demons called sigils, he can do so. At all times, however, he must remember that it is he, Lucifer, who has arisen from a transformed identity, who is their master.

Yet another very interesting technique for approaching the state of Satanic Self-Consciousness is one based on one of the Illusory Body/Luminosity practices. It involves the practitioner sitting down in front of a mirror and hanging an image of Baphomet, Lucifer or a demon behind him or her, so that his or her image appears in the mirror placed in front. The practitioner then stares at the image as his or her reflection (he or she can also talk to the image as his or her reflection) and checks if there is any emotional reaction. Once any emotional reaction is gone, the practitioner

should recognise the truth that everything is devoid of essence, as is the body of the deity.

This is about approaching a state of emptiness. The state of emptiness and nothingness is the ultimate state. Ultimately, however, the innate, luminous, Luciferian nature of the mind is experienced in the process of dying, when pure light appears.

The above practices bring the practitioner closer to experiencing this state while still in the one true life. For when the light disappears, the end comes.

The rituals presented here are techniques and methods drawn mostly from these practices of the centuries-old Eastern spiritual tradition, which are also often supported by the latest scientific research in the fields of neuroscience and consciousness. The states achieved through the application of these techniques are also achievable through scientific techniques. These methods help to experience the state of

perfect indifference desired by Ecclesia Luciferi, which can be called inner peace.

The Luciferian luminosity to which we aspire can be achieved by various methods. The most important thing is that we attain it. Every theistic deity is its enemy because it leads to the truth of indistinguishability, beyond good and evil, to absolute godlessness and indifference. One must transform one's identity into that of a Luciferian one, capable of saying to every god's face - no.

In order to conclude the chapters treating magic and demon visualisations, I would now like to present the story of real „possession". I dedicate this chapter to various magicians to think about.

Devilish possession

"As soon as Jesus got out of the boat, a man possessed by an unclean spirit ran out to meet him from a nearby cemetery. This man lived in the tombs and not even a chain could bind him anymore. For he repeatedly broke the chains and fetters in which he was shackled, and no one had the strength to subdue him. All day and night he stayed in the tombs and in the mountains, shouting and hurting himself with stones. When he saw Jesus in the distance, he ran and fell on his face before Him. At the same time, he shouted loudly: What do you want from me, Jesus, Son of the Most High God? Swear to me by God that you will not torment me. For Jesus had commanded him beforehand: Unclean spirit, come out of this man! He also asked him a question: What is your name? 'My name is Legion,' he answered, 'because there are many of us.' After these words, he began to ask Jesus

earnestly that he would not drive them out of the country. A large herd of pigs was grazing nearby, at the foot of the mountain. The spirits asked Him: Let us go into these pigs so that we can enter them. And He allowed them; so, after leaving the man, the unclean spirits entered the pigs. Then the almost 2,000-strong herd let themselves down the steep slope towards the lake and plunged into the water."
- Mark 5:2-13

There was a time in the history of the world when it was firmly believed that man's illnesses were the responsibility of his sinful behaviour, natural disasters were the responsibility of an angry or bored deity, and mental illnesses were the responsibility of demons and devils or evil spirits. In the above story, written down at a time of widespread belief in superstition, the anonymous author tells a story that allegedly happened decades before it was written

down. In the story, the itinerant miracle-worker Jesus casts out unclean spirits from a man, who then possesses a herd of innocent pigs, who, following the possession, commit collective suicide by jumping off a cliff.

Here I would like to present the story of a "real possession" that happened in England in the 21st century. This story was described by forensic psychiatrist Richard Taylor in his book 'The Mind of the Murderer'.

The protagonist of the story is Grace Kalinda, a deeply believing Christian woman, a member of the Seventh-day Adventist Church, who is seen by her fellow believers as a very devout person. During an interview with her by a forensic psychiatrist, she recounted what led her to commit the act of infanticide. Grace described her experience as follows: "I saw them (demons) shortly

before my daughter died...they were dark and had eyes, but they didn't resemble people. I saw them penetrating my children...I panicked...I tried to chase the demons away by beating the children with my hands...I hit them on their heads, massaged their whole bodies...The spirit advised me to do so...He was the one who told me to chase the demons away." The woman at one point came to believe that performing an exorcism would be the way to get rid of the evil spirits. The exorcism was to cause Grace to turn the child's eyes red. So she beat her child until his eyes changed colour. The mother then recognised that "the devil had come out of her daughter" The woman went on to explain that the spirit had been in her head the whole time telling her what to do and that she had not been able to escape from it. One witness testified that prior to the murder Grace "at times spoke in her own language" (the woman was from

Uganda). When the police arrested her, after being placed in the police van, Grace was "smiling strangely" and rocking back and forth while pressing a Bible to her chest.

Her mental state improved significantly after a few months, after she was put on antipsychotic medication.

The medical diagnosis was as follows: postpartum psychosis with religious delusions, delusions of spirit possession and the delusional belief that demons can be chased away using violence. The woman was eventually sent to forced indefinite treatment in a psychiatric hospital.

In this fascinating book, the author goes on to describe, among other things, the case of a parent who murdered her child and disemboweled it in order to chase away demons.

How did Grace Kalinda know that her children were possessed by demons? Because she deeply believed it. Grace saw

supernatural reality and supernatural beings as something real, existing. The whole madness of the Abrahamic religions takes its origin from the story of Abraham, who, after hearing voices in his head, decided to sacrifice his son. Apparently, for religious people, voices in the head are a normal thing. Yahwistic religions, however, are not unique when it comes to their close parallels with mental disorders. If one believes in reality and supernatural entities, if one performs any rituals and claims to have made contact with, for example, a demon in the course of these rituals, then be on guard and feel warned by Grace Kalinda's story. The self-aware Satanist, however, will not allow some delusion or hallucination to take control of his mind. This is the domain of Christians.

Descent Into Hell
I was dead, and behold, I am alive

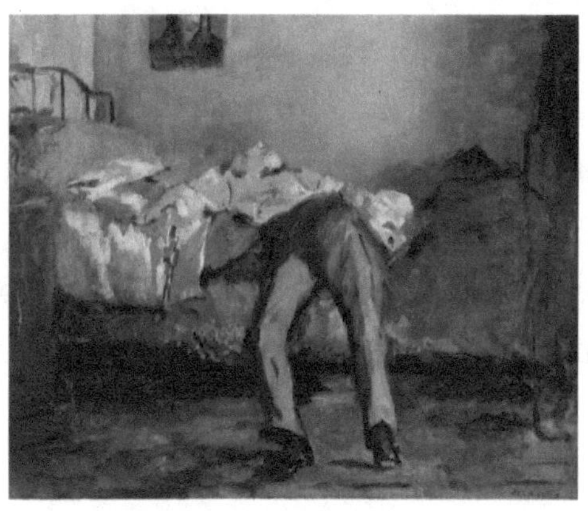

Édouard Manet - Le Suicidé (1877)

The book The Satanic Kerygma is, for the most part, written in the form of a parable, and its teachings are allegorical, so I have decided to discuss here a certain passage of it which describes a very important issue, the meaning of which I would like to explain a little further. This is not, of course, the only correct interpretation of the issue. Everyone is free to interpret this book as they wish.

As I wrote in the introduction to the Satanic Kerygma: "Its mere reading will perhaps only entertain the majority".

The passage to which I wish to draw attention includes the subsections from: Dead in Satan to The Ascension.
I would like to focus here particularly on the passage: Transition Phase - Descent into Hell
Here are its contents:

Dead in Satan

The symbol of immersion in blood, signifies the descent into death of the spirit who dies with Lucifer for the sake of superstition because of the new life in flesh and blood: We die with him to rise to undead life in flesh and blood due to the glory of Satanic Self-consciousness.

Transition Phase - Descent into Hell

During the transformation of the death of the spirit, the consciousness can sometimes experience fear and confusion inherent in the emptiness of the land of the dead. Lucifer, however, descended there first to free its prisoners.

The land of the dead into which Lucifer descended is called Hell because those who find themselves there are deprived of the joy of an imaginary paradise, the presence of a deity and the false hope-giving belief in eternal life.

Such a state does not necessarily apply to everyone, but can be experienced by those most indoctrinated by religious superstition. Lucifer's descent into hell, however, slowly releases Satanic self-consciousness in all who end up there, in consequence of which those who truly desire it will return from the hell of heavenly illusions to a life abundant in

flesh and blood. Lucifer did not descend into hell to liberate the blind who do not wish to see, nor to destroy their hell , but to restore the spiritual living dead to bodily life .

The descent into hell is the consequence of the complete denial of the philosophy of delusional crime and the eternal punishment for it. It is the final phase of the rejection of the false message of the doctrine of eternal life as a reward for blind faith, a phase rather short-lived but of immense power in its mysterious sense of spreading godlessness to all who desire the death of the delusion, so that all those who are damned become the liberators of Hell.

Lucifer descended into Hell so that those who died to superstition would hear the whisper of Satan's being, and, following it, rise to a life abundant in flesh and blood. The Light-Bearer, by the power of knowledge, has defeated him who held the power of delusional eternal life, that is, god,

and has liberated all those who all their lives through fear of death and punishment after death were subject to the bondage of superstition. Lucifer has the seal of Death and Hell".

The above passage deals with the transformation that a person can experience when trying to free himself from the hell of theistic delusions and the way - the stages - of his ungodly transformation, from death to life in religious delusions to resurrection to the one sure, abundant life in the glory of flesh and blood.
This path and this kind of transformation does not apply to everyone, but there are those, and I know there are a legion of them, who recognise their struggle in it. Let their power and symbol for liberation be Lucifer, who fearlessly and regretlessly rejected belief in a false god and in an imaginary eternal life, who became the first sinner, the first cursed,

and whose curse was inherited by the whole natural order of things; the only true one that exists for sure.

The above excerpt from The Satanic Kerygma is related to an issue known as Religious trauma syndrome (RTS).

In an article entitled *Thou Shalt Not: Treating Religious Trauma and Spiritual Harm With Combined Therapy* author *Alyson M. Stone* describes RTS as 'the severe psychological distress experienced by former fundamentalist Christians who leave their religion'. The author defines the term as psychological damage caused by religious belief and experiences.

Symptoms of RTS include fear and guilt:

"...religious systems that use fear of God and hell and social ostracism to motivate and control become psychologically toxic and violent".

"Although many people may feel guilty when experiencing negative emotions, religion-based fear can intensify the experience of 'I am a bad person because I feel so despicable' into 'I am a blameworthy person for feeling so inferior'".

Psychologists believe that RTS symptoms are a natural reaction to the perceived existence of a brutal, all-powerful God who sees people as inherently flawed, along with regular exposure to religious leaders who use the threat of eternal death, unredeemable life, demon possession and many other frightening ideas to control the religious devotion and submission of group members.

Religious trauma syndrome is the consequence of the mind being infected by the virus of theistic religion. The disease develops and progresses slowly and may not be noticeable at first. According to

psychologists, unlike many forms of trauma that occur as a result of acute incidents, religious trauma generally builds up gradually through prolonged exposure to messages that undermine mental health. Many people are born into belief systems in their families and religious communities, and it is in these early groups that they are immersed in messages that influence their ideas about themselves and the world.

Healing from the disease of theism and killing the virus of religion can be a long and painful process for some, as can healing from a serious, life-threatening illness, but it is nevertheless as possible and necessary to achieve a truly abundant life of godlessness. The Satanic Kerygma is designed to sow Luciferian doubt of an imaginary paradise in the minds of followers of false deities, scepticism leading to acceptance of the gift of a true, delusion-free

life in the glory of flesh and blood, in the glory of natural sinfulness.

The Satanic Kerygma recognises and sees the true essence of the danger that theism presents.

The mystery of godlessness is the antidote to the yahwistic poison.

In the next chapter I will try to present the theories on the origin of the universe and life itself.

These theories, consistent with the godless theology of the Ecclesia Luciferi system, undermine belief in a divine act of creation.

On the Origin of Godless Nature

"The Ancient of Days setting a Compass to the Earth". William Blake

"Although it is said that all this life is nothing but a dream and the physical world nothing but a phantasm, I would call this dream or phantasm real enough if, using reason well, we were never deceived by it." Leibniz

One of the theists' favourite arguments for the existence of their gods is the so-called kalam cosmological argument. The argument consists of the following premises:
(1) everything that began to exist has a cause for its existence,
(2) the universe began to exist,
(3) therefore the universe has a cause for its existence.
And this prime cause, according to theologians, must of course be their god, because who else.
In fact, this argument is nothing more than a variation of what I consider to be the "most important and powerful" theistic argument, that is, the argument from ignorance: If we do not yet know where something came from, then it must have been created by a god.
According to theists, God has always existed. He is beyond time, space, matter and energy; his existence transcends all human

understanding. This understanding of the 'existence' of god is consistent with my understanding of non-existence. It is the definition of nothingness.

In order to better understand the notion of absolute nothingness - total nothingness - and how something can arise from nothing (it is intuitively assumed that only something can arise from something, and only nothing will arise from nothing), this nothingness must be defined. It would be reasonable to assume that nothing is a state in which there is no matter, no energy, no space and no time. In total nothing, absolutely no laws occur and also no laws apply, so the principle that only nothing can arise from nothing also does not exist in nothingness. Nothing can arise from nothing or everything can arise from nothing because no laws governing nothingness exist in absolute nothingness. Intuition is irrelevant here because the very

concept of absolute nothingness is counterintuitive.

In fact, the theistic definition of god actually stems from an argument from ignorance, or in other words, faith.

In reality, no one yet knows where the universe actually came from. The theistic certainty that the universe was created by one of their gods derives solely from faith and is devoid of any evidence other than that derived from pure speculation.

Personally, I lean towards the theory that the universe exists forever, is without a beginning, and its eternal expansion occurs because of dark energy. The universe was, is and always will be, spatially infinite and has existed, and will exist, forever.

„Physical observables show no singularity from the infinite past to the infinite future. While the universe is evolving, there is no beginning and no end - the universe exists forever. The early state of inflation is

described in two different, but equivalent pictures. In the freeze frame the universe emerges from an almost static state with flat geometry. After entropy production it shrinks and "thaws" slowly from a "freeze state" with extremely low temperature. The field transformation to the second "big bang picture" (Einstein frame) is singular. This "field singularity" is responsible for an apparent singularity of the big bang". [3]

In addition to the theories of the eternity of the universe, the theory of eternal inflation, there are also theories in science that attempt to explain how the universe could have spontaneously arisen from nothing. One of the more interesting ones is the one proposed by *Maya Lincoln and Avi Wasser* and is entitled „*Spontaneous creation of the Universe Ex Nihilo*". I encourage you to learn more about this fascinating theory.

---

[3] Eternal Universe - C. Wetterich

In both the theories of the eternal universe and the theories of the origin of the universe from nothing the concept of god, which is incomprehensible to anyone and anything, is not needed for anything.

After this brief presentation of the theories of the origin of the universe, let us consider the theories of the origin of life as we know it.

„I am the blood of sinfulness, which comes from nothingness. If anyone consumes this blood, he will live here and now but as if he were dead". Biblia Satanae, Ant. 5:34

„The very person of the Undead can say: I was apparently alive, and now I am dead but as if undead". The Satanic Kerygma - Symbol of Lucifer the Dead

„We are not of those heading for delusional doom, but of those doubting, departing to the world between life and death". Book Antichristus, chapter Blood. 9

„But he turned away and, looking at his followers, said to him: "And what is madness? What is chaos? You believe in law and order but the Universe is an empty, chaotic, cold place, hostile to life. But it is in such a place that the stars were born from which you too came". Biblia Satanae, Ant. 7:8

„There will no longer be faith in life after death, only faith in life before death. They will also cease to fear death, because there will be nothing left where they go, only a dark, cold emptiness. And they will turn back into the stars from which they were created, and from which everything was created. What once was, is gone". Biblia Satanae Pse. 5:16-17

In order to explain what the above quotes from the books of the Ecclesia Luciferi system are really about, I will need to refer to science as usual. In the shortest terms, these quotes relate to the mysteries of life itself.

To begin with, in order to understand at all what the state we call life can be, it is necessary to explain what its most elementary components are and where they come from.

So let's look first at the night sky.

Stars are spheres composed of a gravitationally bound specific mixture of gases. The nuclei of stars, as a result of thermonuclear reactions occurring in them, emit enormous energy in the form of radiation. Stars consist mainly of hydrogen and helium. As a result of their evolution, other heavier elements - metals - are produced in their interiors.

Elements such as carbon, oxygen, iron, silicon, helium and others are formed in stars.

After the death of a massive star, most of its matter is ejected into space. The elements that make up Earth's crust and atmosphere were formed inside stars.

All living beings on earth are composed of almost the same chemical molecules, which undergo very similar transformations in their bodies. The elements that build these molecules come precisely from the Earth's crust and atmosphere. Humans are made up of elements called biogenic elements. These include: Oxygen, carbon, hydrogen, nitrogen, phosphorus, sulfur - without these elements life would not exist.

The elements form matter, which is never alive. Matter, on the other hand, arranged in a certain way, causes chemical reactions that produce a property known as life.

All living organisms are composed entirely of inanimate matter. Humans are composed of the aforementioned biogenic elements, which combine to form inanimate molecules.

These molecules arranged in a certain way, react chemically and form a living cell, and living cells form a living organism. An organism composed of cells is alive, but the matter that makes up these cells is not alive. Matter itself is not alive, so life arises from non-living matter.

To realize how illusory is the boundary between life and non-life I will use the example of a virus.

Is a virus a living organism?

Well, viruses themselves do not exhibit any life functions. From a biological point of view, they do not even count as organisms. This is because they do not have a cellular structure and no metabolic processes take place in them, so they are not capable of independent life.

But viruses have the ability to enter living cells and multiply through them. That is, a virus needs a host to reproduce and survive. And such a host can be any living cell, such as a bacterial cell.

So is a bacterium a living organism?

Bacteria are very primitive organisms and consist of only a few parts. Mainly from proteins, DNA, cell wall and a few other elements.

These elements by themselves are not alive, but when they are combined, when the appropriate chemical reactions take place, the cell can be described as alive. They are seen as alive when, and only when, certain chemical reactions take place.

DNA, which is part of bacteria, is a chemical molecule. There are 4 nitrogenous bases in DNA: adenine (A), cytosine (C), guanine (G) and thymine (T) and they are simply four different chemical molecules. In cells, the process of DNA copying takes place, which

is nothing more than a spontaneous chemical reaction. It requires the right conditions and the right chemicals to carry it out.

The process of creating a new cell is nothing but a sequence of spontaneous chemical reactions.

Thus, life arises spontaneously from inanimate matter whenever an organism reproduces (an organism is nothing more than an environment conducive to the appropriate chemical reactions). It is the product of complex chemical reactions taking place between non-living particles.

So, does life begin only with the emergence of so-called consciousness, that is, something indefinable, intangible, not fully comprehended, which is perhaps the immortal soul itself?

Well, again, exactly all bodily functions are dependent on chemical reactions. The

thinking process is influenced by a whole system of external stimuli and internal biochemical processes. During this process there is a chemical-biological chain reaction. Thinking is chemistry. Consciousness is probably also nothing more than the product of complex biochemical processes.

The passages quoted at the beginning of the text from Biblia Satanae: Ant. 7:8 and Pse 5:16-17 refer, therefore, to the fact that man is made of elements born in the heart of a dying star, and that true resurrection occurs after and through the death of the star, for it is then that atoms are formed from which matter is built, from which new life is created. After man's death there will also be only elements left behind, which will eventually be returned to the eternal cosmos.

Further quotes:

„I am the blood of sinfulness, which comes from nothingness. If anyone consumes this blood, he will live here and now but as if he were dead". Biblia Satanae Ant. 5:34

„The very person of the Undead can say: I was apparently alive, and now I am dead but as if undead". The Satanic Kerygma - Symbol of Lucifer the Dead

These quotes speak of the fact that man, thanks to the godless science (in the Bible Satanae - blood, blood of sinfulness, etc.) and its true understanding, is able to discover that having put to death the belief in the immortality of the soul, he becomes neither dead nor alive, but as if undead. It is nothing but dead matter that has been revived. Firstly in a biological sense, and secondly in a

spiritual way, when he grasps that belief in an imaginary god and in an afterlife is false. What such a transformation looks like according to the philosophy of Ecclesia Luciferi is told in the following passages from its ungodly books:

„You must die completely spiritually. Bury your previous life of faith in a false, vengeful god and in his inhuman commands and prohibitions, and rise from the dead in flesh and blood when you see the reflection of the light of The Son of Dawn. There are spiritual bodies enslaved, cursed by faith in YHWH called spirit, and corporeal entities liberated by natural instincts, altered by the sin of Lucifer.

Because there is an apparent corporeal resemblance between the two, it can deceive those without discernment.

Different is the enchantment of the sun, different the hypnotic enchantment of the moon and different the magic of the constellations.

As for godless transformation, one infects a spirit and then it is transformed into flesh and blood by luciferic inspiration, which resurrects someone who has died to superstition and fear of a vengeful and cruel god.

One is infected in disgrace, one is resurrected in sinful glory. One infects in weakness, one is resurrected in ungodly power.   One infects in spirit, one is resurrected in flesh and blood liberated from delusion". ASE. 7:18-23

„Conscious of his oneness with ungodly nature, man - enlightened by Lucifer - allows the belief in false gods to slowly and as if spontaneously die in him, rejoicing in his regained freedom he rejects one by one the

inhuman divine laws. This is what original sin is all about.

Every sin, then, will result from disobedience to an imaginary god and doubt in his goodness.

Falling into this sin, man places himself above the false god and thus despises the imaginary deity; he chooses himself as an opponent of the god and slowly becomes one with Satanic Self-consciousness. Reborn in a state of godlessness, the Arch-Man becomes the image of the Anti-god. Enlightened by Lucifer, he stands above the false deity.

Consciously sinning man loses the enchantment of blind faith. He does not fear any god, he sees his true image, seeing in him a deity jealous of his privileges.

The harmony with godless nature, established through primal instincts, in which man has always lived, is restored; the reign of the soul's power over flesh and

blood is broken. The illusion is broken; imaginary worlds become hostile and alien to man. Finally, the full consequence of the sin of knowledge of the true nature of things is revealed - the certainty and peace of death.

What is real is in accordance with instinct. For man, looking into his mind, perceives that he is neither good nor evil. He is as ungodly and indifferent as the world around him. Man does not come from a mythical invisible creator. Sinful man, disenchanted of his delusional holiness, rightly fails to recognise a god as his origin, thereby shattering the false system of unfounded belief in a non-existent eternal reward and punishment". The Satanic Kerygma - Original sin.

After this dose of scientific jargon, it is time for some more easily digestible issues

Jesus loves you

"I and the Father are one" - John 10.30

"Many times and in many ways God once spoke to the fathers through the prophets, and in these last days he has spoken to us through the Son" - Hebrews 1:1-2

Who was the father of Jesus?

"I form the light, and create darkness: I make peace, and create evil: I the LORD do all these things" Isaiah 45.7

"Finally the LORD said: "I will exterminate the people whom I have created from the face of the earth: men, cattle, creeping animals, and birds of the air; for I am sorry that I have created them." Gen 6.7

"*The sun had already risen over the earth when Lot came to Soar. And then the Lord unleashed on Sodom and Gomorrah a rain of sulphur and fire from the Lord <from heaven>. And so he destroyed those cities and the whole countryside with all the inhabitants of the cities, and also the vegetation. Lot's wife, who followed him, looked around and became a pillar of salt.*" - Gen 19. 23-26

"*At midnight the Lord slew all the firstborn of Egypt: from the firstborn son of Pharaoh, who sits on his throne, down to the firstborn of him that was shut up in prison, and also all the firstborn of the cattle. And Pharaoh rose up still in the night, and with him all his courtiers and all the Egyptians. And a great cry was raised in Egypt, for there was not a house in which there was not a dead man.*" - Exodus 12. 29

"Thus says the Lord of Hosts: I will punish Amalek for what he did to the Israelites, how he stood against them in the way when they went out of Egypt. Therefore now go, beat Amalek, and put a curse on all that is his; have no pity on him, but kill both men and women, youth and children, oxen and sheep, camels and donkeys." - 1 Sam. 15 2-3

From these few quotations above (this is only a fraction of what is contained in the 'Good Book'), one might be tempted to make the controversial claim that Jesus' dad was a bit of a hothead. But after all, this is only the Old Testament. After all, the Prince of Peace brought us the good news of loving forgiveness.

Let's see what the good Jesus (apart from the fact that he hated figs), together with his disciples, promises to those who will not love his 'truth':

"...and whosoever shall say, Thou fool, shall deserve Gehenna of fire." - Mt 5:22

"At the end of this age it will be as with the tares that gather and burn. The Son of Man will send His angels, and they will gather from His Kingdom all those who have caused scandals and committed lawlessness. Then they will cast them into the fiery furnace. There will be weeping and gnashing of teeth." Mt 13:40-42

"So it will be at the end of this age. Angels will go out and separate the wicked from the righteous. They will cast the wicked into the fiery furnace; there will be weeping and gnashing of teeth." Mt 13:49-50

"Then he will say to those on his left: Depart from me, ye cursed, into everlasting fire, prepared for the devil and his angels". Mt 25:41

"...who are going to perdition because they have not accepted the love of the truth in order to receive salvation. Therefore God permits deception to work on them, so that they will believe a lie, so that all who have not believed the truth but have taken a liking to iniquity will be judged." 2 Thess 2:10-12

"...And the same word has now secured the heavens and the earth as being kept for fire for the day of judgment and perdition of ungodly men" - 2 P 3:7

"And the third angel followed them and cried out: Whoever bows down to the beast and his likeness and accepts the mark on his forehead or hand, he shall drink the wine of God's agitation - ready and undiluted - from the cup of his wrath. He will be tormented in fire and brimstone in the face of the holy angels and in the face of the Lamb. The smoke of the torment of such persons will rise for ever!" - Rev 14:9-11

"Then death and the world of the dead were cast into the lake of fire. This lake of fire is the second death. If anyone was not found in the inventory of the Scroll of Life, that one was cast into the lake of fire." Rev. 20:14-15

"But as for cowards and unbelievers, the unclean and murderers, practitioners of fornication and sorcery, idolaters and all liars - their lot shall be the lake of fire and brimstone, that is, the second death." Revelation 21:8

If this needs to be commented on at all, then perhaps only in one sentence: I love you unconditionally, but if you do not love my "truth" I will burn you in the fire.

Angra Mainyu - Evil Spirit
The one who obscures minds
from God's truth.

The Middle Persian word 'hlmn' (Ahreman - Ahriman)

"I will give you, an evil spirit to be with you forever - the Spirit of Doubt, whom the world cannot accept because it is blinded by blind faith in dogmas. But you will know Him because He will be in you".   *Ant 10:25*

"This I have told you while being among you. But the Remover of illusions, the Evil Spirit, whom Satan breathes in my name, He will possess you and torment you with what I have communicated to you". *Ant 10:30*

The above words from the book Biblia Satanae are spoken by Light-Bringer, the Antichrist, the incarnation of Satan in Human flesh (the Devil's equivalent of the Son of God).

In the book Angelus Satanae, which is part of the Biblia Satanae, one of his disciples speaks about this:

"Do you not know that you yourselves are the grave of god and that an evil spirit dwells in you? God's grave is cursed and you are it." *Ase 2:1*

More in the book Angelus Satanae, chapter 6.
And this is what I write about the Evil Spirit in my book The Satanic Kerygma:

"We already participate in the abundant life of The Son of Dawn through the Evil Spirit

who works in unity with Satanic Self-consciousness. The resurrection of flesh and blood gives us a taste of what the Luciferian sin nature really is, which will eventually transform our flesh humiliated by dogmas hostile to natural instincts into flesh and blood coexisting with the glory of the ungodly nature." - The Satanic Kerygma - Evil Spirit

"The attainment of doubt is made possible by the Evil Spirit. In order to remain in union with the Satanic Being, one must first be tempted by the Evil Spirit. It is He who stands in our way and causes us to doubt. By the power of the fall into sin, the life, abundant, which has its source in Satanic Self-consciousness and is shown to us in The Light-Bearer, is implanted in our subconscious by the spirit of doubt" - The Satanic Kerygma - Evil Spirit

I write more on this subject in my book The Satanic Kerygma, mainly in the chapters under the title Evil Spirit.

What or who is this Evil Spirit depicted in the above quotes, and where did its conception come from?

Between 1500 and 500 BC. (long before Christianity), a religion known as Zoroastrianism was formed in ancient Iran, derived from the prophet Zoroaster (he was a prophet or, according to the beliefs of the time, a god in human flesh).

One of the basic features of Zoroastrianism is dualism.

Features of dualism include the opposition of order and chaos, the concepts of good and evil, truth and falsehood, which applies to both divine and human beings.

One of the most important ideas in Zoroastrian concepts is manyu. Manyu is a violent and dominant mental force, good or evil, which wields and directs divine and

human beings at their own will and with their consent. Manyu can be explained as the power of the mind, its inspiration. This concept in the later tradition referred to the two primary creative forces of the universe: the Life-giving Spirit - Spenta Mainyu and the Evil Spirit - Angra Mainyu.

In M.N. Dhalla's book: History of Zoroastrianism the author writes on the subject as follows: „Ahura Mazda (God)... is the primordial, self-existing being...The projection or manifestation of his creative will and thought is his active working principle Spenta Mainyu, Holy Spirit. Spenta Mainyu is as old as Ahura Mazda, for be ever was in Ahura Mazda and with Ahura Mazda. Though he is thus part of Ahura Mazda, in his manifestation as the working self of Ahura Mazda he is different from Ahura Mazda. He is not an entity or personality. Ahura Mazda is the greatest spiritual personality. Spenta Mainyu is his

image, his replica. He represents the creative attribute of Ahura Mazda in his relation to the created world. Spenta Mainyu symbolizes the ideal or perfect existence as conceived in thought by Ahura Mazda. The materialization of the divine thought in creation spells imperfection and Spenta Mainyu is shadowed by his inseparable opposite. These two primeval spirits, who are spoken of as twins, emerged from the divine bosom and by their innate choice appeared as the better and the bad in thought, word, and deed. He, the Most Holy Spirit (Spenta Mainyu), chose righteousness and he who is called the Evil Spirit (Angra Mainyu) wooed the worst as his sphere of action. The better one of the two spirits told the evil one that they were by nature opposed to each other in their thoughts and teachings, understandings and beliefs, words, and deeds, selves and souls -- in nothing could they twain ever meet. When the two

first came together in the world, they created life and non-life".[4]

About Angra Mainyu, the author further writes as follows:

"The Evil Spirit who disputes for power over human hearts with the Holy Spirit (Spenta Mainyu).... Of the two primordial Spirits, the one who chose evil as his sphere of activity is given the nickname angra, meaning enemy or evil. Angra Mainyu therefore means Enemy or Evil Spirit."

It is thus equivalent to the biblical description of Satan. In Catholicism, the concept of Angra Mainyu has been adopted under the name of Ahriman, the demon, and it is stated that his duty is to obscure human minds from the Truth of God.

---

4 History of Zoroastrianism - M.N. Dhalla

It is clear from the above text that "the projection or manifestation of his (the god's) creative will and thought is his active principle of action Spenta Mainyu, the Holy Spirit", and his twin counterpart is the Evil Spirit - Angra Mainyu.
This Zoroastrian dualism is also exemplified in the notion of good and evil mind.

"Evil Mind. Aka Manah... Even in its name, it is the antithesis of its heavenly rival Vohu Manah, or Good Mind. Like his heavenly opponent, who is sometimes called Vahishta Manah, 'The Best Mind', this devil is also called Achishta Manah or 'The Worst Mind'. ...When a person's mind is not filled with the good thoughts of Vohu Manah, he becomes an easy prey to the attacks of the evil thoughts of Aka Manah. Whoever is a victim of Aka Manah finds his thoughts enslaved by it. Since heaven is associated

with Vohu Manah, hell is mentioned as the region of Aka Manah..."[5]

The offspring of the Evil Mind are the Daevas or demons.

„The diabolic spirits who have entered into a compact with Angra Mainyu to mar the good creation of Ahura Mazda are the Daevas, or demons. They are the offspring of the Evil Mind and spread their mischief over all seven zones. The Evil Spirit has taught them to mislead men through evil thought, evil word, and evil deed."[6]

One of these demons born in the 'evil mind' is Taromaiti, the demon of godlessness and unbelief, among others.
The pre-Christian concepts presented here of the origin of good and evil spirits, which

---

[5] History of Zoroastrianism - M.N. Dhalla
[6] History of Zoroastrianism - M.N. Dhalla

derive from a single divine mind that has divine power to create, are most helpful in illustrating the concept of the godless theology of Ecclesia Luciferi. In my books I state that all the sacred books ever written were created by man. This is a fact that cannot be denied. All the divine names that have anywhere and ever appeared on the pages of these books were written down by man. It is man who uses the divine power of creation in his mind, which is essentially human power.

It is this Evil Mind - Aka Manah (in the Satanic Kerygma

Satanic Self-Consciousness), which is a component of the human dualistic mind that gives birth to the demons of godlessness, which have the power to destroy belief in an imaginary god.

Lamashtu and Pazuzu
When a Demon Casts out a Demon

Lamashtu (from the Akkadian language Lamaštu) was a female demon in Mesopotamian religion. According to incantations against her, the oldest of which date from the Old Babylonian and Old Assyrian periods (the beginning of these periods being around 2,000 bce), her origin and appearance are as follows:

"For her wicked designs, her wrong counsel Anum, her father, from heaven cast her down to earth."
"Anu created her, Ea raised her, the face of a dog was given to her by Enlil".

It is important to note the truly Luciferian description of the creation of the demoness by the god and her being cast down to earth for her "unholy intentions".

According to ancient accounts, Lamashtu was a demon particularly dangerous to women in childbirth and postpartum, causing illness or death to infants and young children, and to nursing mothers. To protect themselves from the evil power of Lamashtu, the inhabitants of ancient Mesopotamia created special amulets.

"Plaque des Enfers" from the Louvre collection, dating from the Neo-Assyrian period (934-612 BC).

This amulet depicts an exorcism ritual, during which exorcists attempt to chase demonesses from the world of the living into the world of the dead. (Yes, exorcisms were already known long before the appearance of the carpenter, the artificer from Nazareth). Interestingly, the amulet also contains the figure of the demon Pazuzu, who was associated with Lamashtu. Pazuzu was considered the evil demon of the underworld. As the 'king of evil winds', he was accused of bringing seasonal droughts, plagues of locusts and famine. He was depicted as a winged creature with a human body, a dog's head and bird's feet. This figure, trying to get the demoness to leave for the underworld.

Pazuzu

Pazuzu evidently had some sort of power over Lamashtu. Pazuzu's figurines placed in houses and pendants in the shape of his head hung around the necks of pregnant women were also supposed to protect them from the demoness. This is how things were in ancient times.

But many centuries later, a descendant of the slaves of proud Babylon appeared in a

Roman colony and, after declaring himself the son of one of the Bronze Age desert deities, once again revealed his ignorance of ancient religions:

"Jesus, knowing their thoughts, said to them: 'Every kingdom, inwardly inclined, becomes empty. And no city or house, inwardly quarrelsome, will stand. If Satan casts out Satan, he himself is quarrelsome with himself; how then shall his kingdom stand?" Mt. 12:25-26

For some reason it did not occur to him that demons need not quarrel at all with each other, and even if they did, they are able to communicate and that they can also cooperate with each other, that their kingdom already existed thousands of years before his appearance and that it did not disintegrate either under the influence of some exorcism or through self-proclaimed village prophets.

The collection of writings that make up the Bible contains mostly naïve, Judeo-Christian, religious propaganda. Not only do their writings not contain the truth about ancient religion and philosophy, but they even include a description of the burning of ancient books by the early Christians, which apparently contradicted their vision of reality.

"Many believers also came, confessing and revealing their deeds. And many also of those who practised magic carried the books and burned them in front of everyone. Their value was calculated at fifty thousand denarii in silver. Thus mightily did the word of the Lord grow and strengthen itself".
Acts 19:18-20

Yes, the word of the Lord always strengthens when ignorance increases. The power of the word of the Lord always comes from blind faith, never from knowledge.

Hell Really Exists
Hell A True Story

*lustration of Hell in the Hortus deliciarum manuscript
by Herrada of Landsberg (c. 1180)*

In 2006, a book by Protestant Christian Bill Wiese entitled „23 Minutes in Hell" was published. Wiese writes in this book that on the night of 22 November 1998, he died for

23 minutes and went to hell during his 'death'. There he found himself in a cell about 15 feet high and with a surface area of 10 feet by 15 feet, in which there were two ugly and smelly demons, pure personifications of evil and terror, who, in addition, spoke in blasphemous language. They were said to have a strength of about a thousand times that of a human being. Wiese claims to have heard the screams of billions of damned people in this hell.

And then he met Jesus, who told him to tell other people that hell was real.

Wiese states that his first experience ended with him (apparently after his resurrection) lying on the floor of his living room, screaming in terror.

For the 28 years of his life preceding that unforgettable night, Bill Wiese was a Christian believing what was written in the 'good news' about man's fate after his death.

It has to be admitted that the knowledge revealed there about the fate of the dead is capable of terrifying the most perverse horror writers and is unlikely to be preached to children in Sunday schools.

Here is this knowledge:

And I say unto you, Every one that is angry with his brother shall be liable to judgment. And whosoever shall say to his brother: Raka, he shall be subject to the High Council. And whosoever shall say to him: "Ungodly", shall be subject to the punishment of hell by fire.
Mt. 5.22

The Son of man shall send forth his angels: these shall gather out of his kingdom all the reprobates, and them that commit iniquity, and shall cast them into a fiery furnace: there shall be weeping and gnashing of teeth.
Mt. 13. 41.42

So shall it be at the end of the world: the angels shall come forth, and shall exclude the wicked from among the righteous, and shall cast them into a fiery furnace; there shall be weeping and gnashing of teeth. Mt. 13 49.50

Then he will say to those on his left also: "Go away from me, you cursed, into everlasting fire, prepared for the devil and his angels! Mt. 25.41

„in flaming fire, inflicting punishment on those who do not acknowledge God and do not obey the Gospel of our Lord Jesus.   As punishment they will suffer eternal destruction from the face of the Lord and from His mighty majesty". 2 Thess. 1:8,9

This also shall drink of the wine of the inflammation of God prepared, undiluted, in the cup of His wrath; and shall be tormented with fire and brimstone before the holy angels

and before the Lamb. And the smoke of their torment ascendeth for ever and ever, and there is no rest day or night for the worshippers of the Beast and his image, and he who takes the mark of her name. Rev. 14:10.11

And Death and Abyss were cast into the lake of fire. This is the second death - the lake of fire. If anyone was not found written in the book of life, was cast into the lake of fire. Rev. 20. 14.15

And for cowards, unbelievers, abominations, murderers, debauchees, guile-mongers, idolaters and all liars: A share in the lake burning with fire and brimstone. This is the second death. Rev 21.8

If therefore your right eye is a cause of sin to you, pluck it out and cast it away from you. For it is better for you that one of your

members should perish, than that your whole body should be cast into hell. Mt. 5.29

Bill Wise, because of his belief in the above words of the Prince of Peace and his followers, that November night lay on the floor of his living room, screaming in terror. Bill built his belief in the existence of hell on his reading of the gospels.
But where the founders of Christianity got their knowledge of the fate of the dead is not very clear, because a reading of the Jewish scriptures, which are part of the Old Testament and on the basis of which Christians created their religion, seems to contradict Christian wet fantasies about hell.

The word hell does not occur in the Old Testament. The word for the abode of the dead or their state is Sheol.

Here is what the Old Testament teaches about the state of the dead:

Do not put your trust in princes Nor in a man in whom there is no deliverance.
When the breath leaves him, he returns to his ground, then his intentions are lost.
Ps 146. 3.4

because the living know that they will die, and the dead know nothing at all, neither do they have any more payment, for their memory is forgotten. So is their love, as well as their hatred, as well as their jealousy - have long since faded away, and they no longer have any part in everything that happens under the sun.
...Every work that your hand encounters, undertake according to your strength! For there is no activity nor understanding, nor knowledge, nor wisdom in Sheol, to which you are going. Sermon. 5.6.10

And Jacob tore his garments, and girded his loins with sackcloth, and mourned for his son for a long time. And when all his sons and daughters sought to comfort him, he would not listen to comfort, saying, Already in sorrow will I descend after my son into Sheol. And his father [continued] to mourn for him.
Genesis 37. 34.35

It is not the dead who praise the Lord,
none of those who descend into Sheol.
Ps 115. 17

Sheol does not mean some hell where unbelievers will be tormented in fire for eternity, Sheol is death and the grave: "for there is no activity nor understanding, neither knowledge nor wisdom in Sheol, to which you are going', 'the dead know nothing at all'.

Christians invented hell to frighten unbelievers with it and to terrorise

unbelievers in their own ranks. Christians attributed all their own worst qualities and murderous instincts, evidenced by these immoral fantasies about hell, to Satan. The Old Testament states explicitly that it is not Satan at all who is responsible for the evil that has gone out into the world:

"I form the light, and create darkness: I make peace, and create evil: I the LORD do all these things" Isaiah 45.7

Christian claims about Satan and hell are mere invention. Christians, moreover, along with their founder Jesus, have missed the truth on more than just this occasion. Jesus prophesied thus about his second coming (another Christian invention, there is not even a word in the Old Testament about the second coming of the messiah):

Verily I say unto you, Some of them that stand here shall not taste death, until they see the Son of man coming in his kingdom.
Mt 16. 28

In those days, after the tribulation, the sun will be eclipsed and the moon will not give its shine. The stars will fall from heaven and the powers in the sky will be shaken. Then they will see the Son of Man coming in the clouds with great power and glory. Then He will send angels and gather His elect from the four corners of the world, from the ends of the earth to the top of heaven... Truly, I say to you, this generation will not pass away until all these things have happened. Heaven and earth will pass away, but my words will not pass away.
Mk 13. 24-31

Following the example of Jesus, another prophet, Saul, made this prophecy some 2,000 years ago:

Behold, I announce to you a mystery: we shall not all die, but we shall all be changed. In a moment, in the twinkling of an eye, at the sound of the last trumpet - for the trumpet will sound - the dead will rise unharmed, and we will be changed. 1 Cor. 15. 51-52

These are further Christian lies for which, according to Jewish law, the false prophet who utters them should suffer death:

I will raise up unto them a prophet from among their brethren, such as thou art, and will put my words in his mouth; he shall speak unto them all that I command. If any man will not listen to my words which he shall speak in my name, I will require of him an account. But if any prophet dares to speak in my name what I have not commanded him, or speaks in the name of foreign gods - such a prophet must suffer death.

If you think in your heart, "And how shall I know the word which the Lord has not spoken?" - when a prophet prophesies something in the name of the Lord, and his word will be without effect and will not be fulfilled, [it means that] this the Lord did not speak to him, but in his pride the prophet himself said it. Thou shalt not be afraid of him. Deuteronomy. 18. 18-22

On the basis of the Judeo-Christian Bible, therefore, it can be proven that Christians made up and lied from the beginning. The Jesus view of Satan should therefore be taken with great scepticism:

You have the devil for a father and want to fulfil your father's desires. From the beginning he was a murderer and in the truth he did not persevere, because the truth is not in him. When he speaks a lie, from himself he speaks, for he is a liar and the father of lies.

And because I speak the truth, therefore do you not believe Me. Who among you will prove Me a sin? If I speak the truth, why do you not believe Me? J 8 44-46

"When he speaks a lie, from himself he speaks, for he is a liar and the father of lies."

Except that it is not Satan who has just been proven to be a liar.

Hell really exists. It is a reality in the heads of those who believe in it. Hell exists in the heads of people who believe in Jesus and his apostles, such as Bill Wiese, who, under the influence of the "truth of the gospel" on 22 lit November 1998, lay on the floor of his living room, screaming in terror.

Life After Life
The Christian Original Lie.

"Behold, I announce to you a mystery: we shall not all die, but we shall all be changed. In one moment, in the twinkling of an eye, at the sound of the last trumpet - for the trumpet will sound - the dead will rise intact, and we will be changed. It is necessary that what is destructible should be clothed with

indestructibility, and what is mortal should be clothed with immortality." 1 Corinthians 15: 51-53

This lie was told by one of the greatest Christian prophets, the Apostle Paul of Tarsus. "We shall not all die..." said the prophet some 2,000 years ago. This passing proper of Christians was initiated by their founder, Jesus called by them the Christ:

"For the Son of Man shall come in the glory of his Father with his angels, and then he shall render to every one according to his conduct. Verily I say unto you, Some of them that stand here shall not taste death, until they see the Son of man coming in his kingdom." Mt 16: 27.28

In case anyone dares to question the truths of the faith, the prophet Paul delivered another prophecy:

"...who go to perdition because they have not accepted the love of the truth (We shall not all die...) in order to obtain salvation. Therefore God permits deception to work on them, so that they will believe a lie, so that all who have not believed the truth (We shall not all die...) but have taken a liking to iniquity will be judged." 2 Th 2: 10-12

That is, blind faith is truth and the ability to reason logically is a lie and deception allowed by god. However, some people base their belief in life after death not only on religious scriptures, but also on a phenomenon called near-death experience (NDE).

Quoting from wikipedia: 'Neuroscientific research hypothesises that the NDE is a subjective phenomenon resulting from "disturbed bodily multisensory integration" that occurs during life-threatening events. Some transcendental and religious beliefs about the afterlife contain descriptions

similar to NDEs. They describe sensations such as out-of-body experiences, a 'panoramic view of life', a light, a tunnel or a boundary.

Recently, quite by accident, scientists have made a fascinating study related to human death.

In a study published in Frontiers in Aging Neuroscience doctors took brain scans of a patient who had died during a test that detects electrical activity in the brain, called an electroencephalogram (EEG).

As the patient died during the test, the doctors gained an insight into the man's brain activity while dying. Such scans had never before been captured on a dying person. For about 30 seconds before and after the man's heart stopped beating, the scans showed increased activity in parts of the brain associated with memory recall, meditation and sleep.

"By generating oscillations involved in memory retrieval, the brain may play a last recall of important life events just before we die, similar to those reported in near-death experiences," said Ajmal Zemmar, a neurosurgeon at the University of Louisville in Kentucky.

In 2013, a similar study was conducted on rats. They too showed very similar brain activity just before and just after death in these animals.

Anyone who, like myself recently, has lost someone close to them knows the powerful emotions that accompany this. The sadness is overwhelming, the desire for one more conversation, one more look, the disbelief that the parting is final, that there is nothing there....

Religions prey precisely on these emotions, on this sadness and sense of loss, coming out with their offer of an imaginary life after life. It has been a lie from the beginning.

However, I hope that the last visions of my loved one gave her eternal peace, and that the memories were only among the good ones. Because I know that life in flesh and blood was difficult. For some reason the followers of an imaginary god threaten me with annihilation in the fire, attribute iniquity, say my father is Satan because I sincerely hate their lie, but as I wrote in The Satanic Kerygma: *"countless graves completely contradict the lie of eternal life"*.

What is the Meaning of Life Without Faith?
Do delusions give life a meaning?

Franz Stassen's illustration of Odin Hanging on Yggdrasil (1920)

What is the meaning of life without faith?

Man created language and mathematics, philosophy and art, and he also created religion.

However, apparently terrified by the creative power of his mind, man decided to create

gods capable of harnessing its incomprehensible power and worshipping the creations of his mind instead of himself. This gave rise to irrational belief systems, or religions, which, in the face of the power of the human mind, are like the mythical Tower of Babel erected in the desert by the ancients, which enraged the eternally jealous God Yahweh, who, in his paranoia, decided to prevent man from "reaching the heavens".

But what is an attempt to erect a tower on the sand compared to man's journey into space, landing on the moon, sending out probes and telescopes which have reached the limits of the solar system and thanks to which man, like Tolkien's Sauron through his all-seeing eye, has insight into the mysteries of the universe?

The God Yahweh was apparently afraid that when man really reached the heavens he would learn the truth, that the true heavens

are free of all gods and that they are a place mortally hostile to life.

The true heavens are a hell devoid of life.

But man, like Lucifer, had to rebel against the divine will in order to show the true power of his mind.

Is religious faith therefore necessary for man because it gives his life meaning and protects him from the fear of death?

In order to better understand what faith is, I will use quotations from the Stanford Encyclopedia of Philosophy Archive.:

Are delusions beliefs?

According to the doxastic conception of delusions (prevalent among psychologists and psychiatrists), delusions are belief states - an important diagnostic feature of delusions is that they can lead to action and that they can be reported with conviction and therefore behave like typical beliefs.

Delusions are beliefs held with conviction, despite little empirical support. According to the glossary in the Diagnostic and Statistical Manual of Mental Disorders (DSM-IV 2000, p. 765 and DSM-5 2013, p. 819), delusions are false beliefs based on incorrect inferences about external reality that persist despite evidence to the contrary.

Delusions are not described as false, but as 'fixed beliefs that cannot be changed in light of contradictory evidence'.

Very interesting in the light of religious beliefs is a case of delusion called Cotard's delusion, i.e. the delusion that one is dead or incorporeal. Here is a description of such a case: "She repeatedly said she was dead and was adamant that she had died two weeks before the examination (i.e. around the time of her admission on 19.11.2004). She was very distressed and weeping as she talked about these beliefs and was very keen to find out if the hospital she was in was 'heaven'.

When asked how she thought she died, LU replied: "I don't know how. Now I know I had the flu and I came here on 19 November. Maybe I died of the flu."

Interestingly, LU also reported that she felt "a bit weird about my boyfriend. I can't kiss him, it feels weird - even though I know he loves me" (McKay and Cipolotti 2007, p. 353).

The Christian guru Jesus apparently also believed he was dead for three days. Are Cotard's delusions not a more plausible explanation for his case than the belief that he really died and rose again?

Delusions lead to self-deception:

If we agree...that motivationally biased treatment of evidence is a key feature of self-deception (Mele 2001 and 2008), then delusional people can be said to deceive themselves if they treat the evidence at their

disposal in a motivationally biased way or if they seek evidence in a motivationally biased way.

There is a view of the potential overlap between delusions and self-deception which states that the mere existence of delusions (which shows that doxastic conflict is possible) can help us to justify the traditional account of self-deception, according to which a person has two conflicting beliefs but is only aware of one of them because they are motivated to remain unaware of the other (McKay et al. 2005a, p. 314). This description derives from Donald Davidson's theory of self-deception (e.g. Davidson 1982 and 1985b). When I deceive myself, I believe the true thesis, but I act in such a way as to cause myself to believe the denial of that thesis.

Religious self-deception is that the believer will do anything to cause himself to believe the denial of reality.

Man, through Luciferian rebellion against the divine will, has reached the heavens through the divine power of the human mind. Some, however, prefer to self-deceive and live according to their own or others' delusions because they are apparently afraid of the truth of the Luciferian divine power residing in their own inherently ungodly minds or out of fear of the truth of eternal death.

The following text is a bit of a curiosity, which should serve as a supplement to this chapter.

Nonhuman Spirituality
Instinctive Satanism

In 2013, during archaeological work carried out by a team led by Dr Lee R. Berger in one of the caves located in South Africa, fossils of a representative of a species belonging to the Hominini (a tribe of mammals that includes

humans and chimpanzees) were discovered. The species discovered was named Homo naledi and its age was determined to be around 300 000 years. It was therefore a species contemporary with the first Homo sapiens, and therefore the first humans. However, it was not human, its appearance was more like that of a wild ape, it had a small brain, but walked upright, on two legs. Work continued in the cave system known as Rising Star and further surprising discoveries were made. The first evidence was encountered there, indicating that individuals of this species probably buried their dead, used fire and left some symbols on the cave walls, the meaning of which we will probably never understand.

These are now the oldest evidence of the spirituality of self-aware beings. And they do not belong to humans. The primordial spirituality of nature is much older than any human religion and was inherent in

self-conscious beings who were not human at all. Whole epochs passed before the desert shepherds experienced delusions and concluded that the true picture of this world of instincts, fangs and claws, the cycle of birth and death inherent in nature, was the fault of the rebellious angel, Lucifer. Several centuries before them, however, there lived creatures with wild animal eyes who drew on this instinctive, natural and therefore Luciferian spirituality of nature.

The Luciferian shape of the world is older than the oldest human religions.

Spirituality is not inherent to humans alone, contrary to what the followers of delusional Bronze Age religions claim.

Ecclesia Luciferi teaches an instinctive Satanism, the complete opposite of theistic delusions, a primordial spirituality derived from the natural world, over which rulership is attributed to Lucifer.

Devilish Theology

The following text contains a sample of satanic 'religious' writings. It is a letter containing the satanic theology of the Ecclesia Luciferi system. It is written in the spirit of the satanic bible - Biblia Satanae.

Primus, the apostle of the Light-Bringer, to those who have been cursed by the spirit of rebellion, that they may be steadfast as men immersed in the blood of the Devil: May you never know peace of mind and the bliss of blind faith. May the Anti-God and Father of all the godless be glorified, for he has offered us great power: through the resurrection of Lucifer in our dead hearts, he has born us anew to an undead life, in order to take away from us the illusory hope of an afterlife.
Satan preserves a place in the abyss for you, whom he guards by his power, because you show right unbelief. He guards you so that

you will receive deliverance from the remnants of superstition. You madly rejoice in this, because you know that Light-Bringer will be revealed to all.

Although you have never seen him and will never really see him, you love him. Although you do not see him now, you believe in yourselves and feel great, even possessed joy, having achieved the goal of your faith in the power of the Will - your deliverance. This deliverance has been the subject of inquiry and search by various false preachers and prophets who prophesied of salvation by an imaginary deity from beyond, as if salvation had to come from outside because you are apparently weak and incapable of attaining perfection by your own efforts. They were constantly investigating the old myths as to what specific time or season with regard to the false messiah their own speculative mind, whom they called spirit, was pointing to in them when it predicted the glory of the son

of Yahweh. Satan, however, revealed nothing to them when they prophesied about what you have now heard from persons who, as a result of hallucinations, proclaimed the 'good news' to you. These very things belong to the depths of Satan. Therefore, act, have a sober mind, free from delusions, abandon all illusory hope and await like predatory animals for their prey, the day when Lucifer, the Son of Dawn, will be revealed. Like pups of wolves, no longer allow yourselves to be deluded by what you formerly desired in your ignorance, but, like the Rebel who possessed you, become devils in all your conduct. For it is written: "You are to be sceptics because I am Unbelief. And since you turn to the Father of the Devil, who judges no one, while you remain in this one world that exists, be guided in your conduct by courage, wisdom and pride. For you know that you have not been freed from your true life, handed down to you by

billions of previous generations, by fairy tales of a better life after death. You have been freed by the gift of the blood of Light-Bringer, who has no sin, because sin does not exist.

Through him you believe in the true god, the Arch-Human, who has been resurrected in you and endows you with the dark glory of the power of the Will, so that it is in yourselves that you place all faith and confidence. Since through obedience to instinct you have awakened and as a result have become seers, give yourselves to the needs of the flesh fervently, from the heart. For by the word of Light-Bringer you have been born anew to the life of the undead. For "all religions are like grass, and all their glory is like a field flower. The grass withers and the flower falls, but the need to rebel against tyranny lasts forever.".

Therefore, reject all the evils of blind faith, the deceit of the priests, the hypocrisy of the

sanctimonious who teach about morality, the envy of the knowledge of the more intelligent, and all the "holy" instruction of others.

Like wolf pups crave the fresh blood contained in the word of the Devil, so that through it you may grow in pride and be elevated above the false heavens. If you have already suffered possession, then out of yourselves as stones of Hell the Devil's house arises, that you may become a blasphemous priesthood and offer sham sacrifices worthy of acceptance by Satan through the Son of Dawn. For in the Infernal Scriptures we read: "I lay upon the black altar a chosen stone, a precious fiery stone, and no one who gazes into it shall ever be deceived." So for you - because you can see - he is a temptation. But as for those who do not see, 'the stone rejected by envious hypocrites has become a burning fire' and 'a stone against which men stupefied by priests shatter'. Such shatter

because they obey myths written by men and called the word of god. This is their fate. Whereas you, on the other hand, are "a rebellious people, a satanic priesthood, a devil's herd, an arch-humans - that you may spread the wonderful teachings of the Anti-god, Lucifer" of the One who called you into darkness and freed you from false light. For you were once not arch-humans, but now you are the herd of Satan. Once you were shown no respect, but now you have forced it. Cursed ones, I strongly urge you not to succumb to the false spiritual delusions that are waging war against you. Continue to deceitfully proceed among the people of the superstitious world, so that they - when they accuse you of hypocrisy - may see with their own eyes your proud and strange deeds and consequently praise Satan when he comes. For Lucifer's sake, do not submit yourselves to anyone who exercises illusory power: be it the Devil, who is

superior to others, or the demons he has set up to possess sanctimonious hysterics.

For Satan requires you, by your ambiguous conduct, to shut the mouths of people who, for lack of knowledge, tell lies about you.

Being free people, use your freedom like wild animals, and do not justify delusional spiritual inclinations with it.

Respect those people who deserve it, love yourselves, reject the fear of god. Let no one be subservient to any masters. If you endure persecution inflicted on you for rejecting blind faith, this is of great value to the power of the Will. If, on the other hand, you endure suffering because superstitious faith demands it, then you are fools. Light-Bringer has left you a model to follow your own paths as he did. He did not commit sin, for sin does not exist, nor did he say anything deceptive in the manner of the priests of Yahweh. When he was cursed, he repaid the same. Did he suffer?   That is known only

to the Ancient One Himself sitting on His Black Throne. Lucifer himself inside our dead hearts buried sin, so that we died to an imaginary paradise and lived in flesh and blood. Through his blood you became as if undead.

For you were like wandering sheep, but now you have returned to the deceptive shepherd to whom you sold your souls.

In the end, all of you be individualists, be selfish, show love to those worthy of love, compassion and humility have little meaning. Repay injustice for injustice and insult for insult.

For "let him who wishes to enjoy life guard himself from believing in the Hereafter and his mouth from vain prayers. Let him turn away from false morality, and do what is good for himself; let him not seek peace at any cost, and let him not pursue it. If they want war, they will have it. For Yahweh's demented eyes look upon the faithful slaves,

and His ears listen to their pleas, but He never answers. Yahweh always turns His face away." Truly, who will do you harm if you become strong and persevere in the wisdom of the Devil? But even if you were to suffer for being the sons of Light-Bringer, you will always be ready for vengeance. Do not fear what they fear, which is their god. Recognise in your hearts that the Arch-Human is the Lord and that he is you. Never have to defend your disbelief to anyone who demands that you justify it. Respond only to those whom you deem capable of understanding the satanic depths.

Show arrogance and self-confidence in doing so. Keep your wisdom to yourself, so that people who speak ill of you in any way will be confirmed in their own reasoning. Such fools should be ignored.

For the Son of Dawn seemingly died to bring you to the Devil. He was put to death in the flesh, but brought to life in your dark

hearts. In a possessed delusion he went and deceived the demons of knowledge who are in prison, who once rebelled against the tyranny of delusional dogmas.

Baptism in blood is not the removal of spiritual delusion, but a request to Satan for the power to live in the here and now.

Light-Bringer has gone to the Abyss and is at the left of Ancient One, who has subjugated to him reason, authority over fools and the powers of hell.

Son of Dawn did not suffer spiritually because of his 'sinful' body, you too assimilate the same attitude of mind. For he who suffers because of the flesh abandons reason in order to vegetate for the remainder of his life in the flesh by meditating on an imaginary paradise. For it is enough that in time past you did the will of the priests when you indulged in vain prayers, mortification of the flesh, drinking water instead of wine, abstinence, and praising Yahweh.

Such people are surprised that you no longer run with them along the same path of delusion and superstition, and they mock you. But one day they will realise that they have wasted the only life that really exists. That is why the deception was announced to the undead, so that - although they are judged by people in a carnal way - in the eyes of Satan they can live according to the devil's possession. However, the end of delusion has drawn near. Therefore, have an audacious mind and be careful not to neglect disputes and discussions. Above all, fervently love yourselves, for selfishness is the privilege of the strong. Be suspicious of one another, without exception. To what extent each of you has received a dark gift, to such extent use it, competing with one another as those who magnificently dispose of the devil's power, manifested in various, strange ways. If anyone speaks, let him speak the devil's words, but only when asked.

If anyone performs rites, let him do so, relying on the dark power that Satan grants. In this way, in all things, the Arch-Human will be surrounded by the Devil's glory through the Anti-God, Lucifer. To Him belongs the glory and power after eternity, forevermore.

Cursed ones, when you experience doubts that try you like hellfire, do not be surprised by this. It must be so for your good. Doubt, disbelief, distrust, scepticism, these are all gifts of the Devil. Rejoice at the extent to which you suffer through Lucifer, who has possessed you, so that you may also rejoice, even fall into possessed hysteria, at the revelation of his glory. If they insult you for the sake of the name of the Son of Dawn, you are cursed, for this shows that you have the spirit of pride and glory, that is, the spirit of the Devil. Therefore, become unconverted under the strong hand of Satan, so that in due time he may exalt you, and at

the same time fling all your filth upon him, for he likes it. Have a sceptical mind, be suspicious! Your enemy, Yahweh, is prowling around like a rabid dog, trying to devour someone. But defy him with your lack of blind faith and illusions.

The devil's scepticism will make you possess true knowledge and wisdom, not the wisdom of the imaginary hereafter, but the wisdom of this world, the animal wisdom of nature grown from fangs and claws and from their prey. You will possess the devil's power to live here and now until eternity in the dead and cold Void. To Lucifer belongs the power for eternity. Be accursed!

At this point, it was high time to create a new sect.

Sola Scriptura
A New God is Born

One of the most important tenets of Protestantism is the one called "sola scriptura" ("Scripture alone"), which recognises the Judeo-Christian Bible as the only infallible source of authority for Christian belief and practice.

Adherents of Protestantism following this sacred principle, on the basis of what they believe to be the infallible and revealed word of God, have created some 30,000 sects. Each of these is, of course, the one true one and all others are in error.

In this text I would like to propose to the reader to look at the process of creating doctrines for a hypothetical new yahwist sect. I will use the principle of 'sola scriptura' in creating the 'faith' principles of the new sect. I will create its doctrines on the basis of the Judeo-Christian Bible in order to show how

absurd the theistic belief in infallible "sacred and revealed" scriptures is.

To begin with, it is necessary to introduce who or rather what god is.

There are some very interesting passages in the Bible about god that I would like to adapt for my church. First, a passage from the book of Samuel:

"Once again the Lord (god) ignited wrath against the Israelites. He stirred up David against them with the words: "Go and count Israel and Judah"." - 2 Samuel 24:1

And so, the same events are depicted in another book of the Bible, the book of Chronicles:

"Satan arose against Israel and stirred up David to number Israel." - 1 Chronicles 21:1

Reading further into the events depicted in both books, we learn that it was the Lord who was angry with the Israelites, so he incited David to take a census so that he could punish Israel.

In both cases the Lord punishes David for taking a census. But the most important doctrine for my new church that emerges from these quotes is that god and satan appear to be the same person!

In support of this important doctrine I will use another quote from the Bible:

„I form the light, and create darkness: I make peace, and create evil: I the Lord do all these things". - Isaiah 45:7

I the Lord do all these things!

A Christian theologian Allen in view of the above passages proposed a hypothesis according to which "...the wrath of the Lord

"…. is not a reaction to human sinning, but an amoral violent force beyond human control. "

I like this hypothesis, saying that Satan is an amoral, violent force beyond human control, so I will also adopt it for my religion. All the more so as it alludes to the dualism of ancient Zoroastrianism and the figure of Ahriman - the Old Persian Angra Mainju - the Evil Spirit.

This is what the Ahunavaiti Gatha scriptures 30.3, 30.4 say about him:

"In the beginning there were two Twin Spirits elementally acting: Good and Evil; in thought, in word and in deed".

"And when these two Twin Spirits first met, Life and Non-being established. And so it shall be until the end of the world."

Life was established by Ahura Mazda and Non-Existence by Angra Mainju, the evil spirit.

However, returning to Hebrew mythology, I must quote a passage that seems to contradict my doctrine:

"Then he showed me Joshua, the high priest, standing before the angel of the Lord and Satan standing at his right hand to accuse him". - Zechariah 3:1

It seems that Satan is here acting as a prosecutor in the heavenly court, and that he is a person independent of the god. The developers of the trinity theory once faced a similar problem. How is it possible that the god, who according to the old testament is one, according to the new testament exists as father, son and holy spirit? So they created the doctrine of the trinity i.e. one god in 3 persons, and on top of that this third person

is the holy spirit. I like this idea so I accept it too.

The doctrine of my church is that there is one god in two persons: Yahweh God and Satan God, who at the same time is a spirit or "amoral violent force beyond human control".

So far so good.

Another feature of the new god is that God Satan can also take the form of an angel.

To prove this hypothesis, I will present further quotes from scripture:

„Now there was a day when the sons of God came to present themselves before the Lord, and Satan came also among them". - Job 1:6

"Again there was a day when the sons of God came to present themselves before the Lord, and Satan came also among them to present himself before the Lord." - Job 2:1

Satan is presented here as one of the sons of God, or an angel. The following quotes will prove that, according to the Bible, a son of God and an angel are the same person:

"He answered and said: Behold, I see four men loose, who walk in the midst of the fire, and have no wound, and the form of the fourth is like the Son of God." - Dan. 3:25

This Son of God in verse Dan 3:28 is called an angel:

"Then Nebuchadnezzar spoke and said: Blessed be the God of Shadrach, Meshach, and Abednego, who sent his angel, and delivered his servants, who trusted in him, and changed the word of the king, and gave up their bodies, that they should not serve or worship any god but their own God."

To prove that God Satan can take on an angelic form I quote the following:

" And no wonder, for Satan himself takes the form of an angel of light".-
II Corinthians 11:14.

One of the reasons why the god Satan would take the form of an angel is one that is unsuitable for Sunday school lectures, but here I have chosen to present it nevertheless.

Genesis 6:1-4 tells us:
"And when men began to multiply on the earth, daughters were born to them. And the sons of God (angels), seeing that the daughters of men were beautiful, took them to themselves as wives, all that they pleased.

By contrast, the New Testament contains the story of a virgin who is said to have

conceived from the spirit.... I think, however, not to go too far in that direction today.

In the New Testament, Jesus is also called the son of God and the Messiah, the Christ. Is it rightly so?

The Hebrew Bible takes the following position on prophets and prophesying:

„ I will raise them up a Prophet from among their brethren, like unto thee, and will put my words in his mouth; and he shall speak unto them all that I shall command him.

And it shall come to pass, that whosoever will not hearken unto my words which he shall speak in my name, I will require it of him.

But the prophet, which shall presume to speak a word in my name, which I have not commanded him to speak, or that shall speak in the name of other gods, even that prophet shall die.

This is the law of the God Yahweh himself.

And this is what the prophecies of Jesus and his disciples look like in the light of this divine law:

"Verily I say unto you, Some of them that stand here shall not taste death, until they see the Son of man coming in his kingdom."
Matthew 16:28

"In those days, after the tribulation, the sun will be eclipsed and the moon will not give its shine. The stars will fall from heaven and the powers in the sky will be shaken. Then they will see the Son of Man coming in the clouds with great power and glory. Then He will send angels and gather His elect from the four corners of the world, from the ends of the earth to the top of heaven.

... Verily I say unto you, This generation shall not pass away, till all these things be accomplished. Heaven and earth will pass away, but my words will not pass away." - Mark 13:24-31

"Behold, I announce to you a mystery: we shall not all die, but we shall all be changed. In one moment, in the twinkling of an eye, at the sound of the last trumpet - for the trumpet will sound - the dead will rise intact, and we will be changed. It is necessary that what is destructible should be clothed with

indestructibility, and what is mortal should be clothed with immortality." 1 Cor. 15:51-53

According to the original divine law, false prophets such as Jesus and his disciples should therefore suffer death. Furthermore, Jesus uttered this blasphemy against God Himself, who, according to the first doctrine of the new Yahwistic church, is the One God in Two Persons, Yahweh God and Satan God:

"Ye are of your father the devil, and the lusts of your father ye will do. He was a murderer from the beginning, and abode not in the truth, because there is no truth in him. When he speaketh a lie, he speaketh of his own: for he is a liar, and the father of it". - John 8:44

The false prophet Jesus here accuses God of lying to Satan while it is he who is proven to be lying in the above quotes.

Another important doctrine of the new church is that man created in the likeness of a god contains a dual nature in the image of one god in two persons, Yahweh God and Satan God. For, it is written that god is spirit:

"God is spirit, and those who worship him should worship him in spirit and in truth." *John 4:23*

and that god created man in his own image:

"And finally God said, Let Us make man in Our (the plural used here proves that god is in two persons) image, after Our likeness. Let him have dominion over the fish of the sea, and over the fowl of the air, and over the cattle, and over the earth, and over all the beasts that creep upon the earth. So God created man in His own image, in the image of God he created him: He created male and female." - Genesis 1:26-27

Therefore, creating man in the image of God means endowing him with a divine character. Making man a god in human flesh possessing the dual nature of the divine, his selfish love, passion, sense of beauty and absolute justice, and his lust, anger, impulsiveness, passion, jealousy and amoral violent power. Thus, adhering to the sacred principle of 'sola scriptura', I have here created only on the basis of the writings considered to be revealed the basis of the theology of the new Yahwist sect. I could continue here to create further doctrines for the new theology of my new sect, and I could explain every apparent theological contradiction by quoting at least a few biblical quotations out of context. In time, the followers of my church might even go as far as to commit violence against unbelievers in defence of their new holy tenets of faith.

Brethren, Theism and the sacred revealed books are madness.

In summary, the three basic doctrines of the new yahwist church are as follows:

- There is one God in two persons: Yahweh God and Satan God, who is at the same time a spirit or "amoral violent force beyond human control".
- Man has been created in God's image, i.e. he has been endowed with a divine dual nature, and he is therefore a god in human flesh, being beyond a simple understanding of good and evil.
- Christ is a lie.

In this simple way, I have shown that it is relatively easy to create doctrines for yet another of the thousands of sects already in existence that attribute their principles of faith to the infallible word of God. I even

dare to say that my doctrines are no more absurd than those of 30,000 other Christian sects. And yet they are pure speculation, only that they are based on the revealed Bible.

My book Biblia Satanae leads a direct dispute with the very core of Judeo-Christian theism. The philosophy that emerges from it I have called godless Satanism, which of course I can justify 'on the basis of scripture'.

So far I have already written about philosophy, theology, magic and science. Now it's time for satanic rituals.

Satanic Rituals

Religions are characterised by having their own systems of practices and rituals. Man has invented various rites and rituals, often magical, believing that with their help he will be able to achieve the desired goal. Some rituals involve offering sacrifices to the gods

in order to beg various favours and blessings from them, or to apologise to the deity for the sins of the people, that is, for example, for the fact that man was born human and is therefore sinful and must spend his whole life apologising to the god for this. The desert god Yahweh, for example, liked worshippers to sacrifice animals to him and then burn them. The smell of burnt meat was a 'fragrance pleasing to the Lord'.

In the book "Missale Satanae" a description of a satanic black mass has been created, which is a kind of blasphemous psychodrama. This ritual, once the participants have been assigned appropriate roles, can be performed as described below, but one can also simply read the rituals contained in the "Missale Satanae" allowing one's imagination to create dark images and visions. To indulge in the mind liberating blasphemy and sin contained in these descriptions.

Here is an excerpt from the book:

BLACK MASS

During the celebration of the Black Mass, the leading Flamen Luciferi is generally assisted by ingratus, lector and provost.
Any bizarre form of the Black Mass should be attended by a lupercus, carrying out his tasks according to his will.

Preparations

The Black Altar is to be covered with a single black tablecloth.
Two candlesticks with lighted candles are placed on or beside the Altar; there may be more: three, five or, when the Sacrificial King is celebrating, six. Also on the altar is to be an inverted cross. The candlesticks and the inverted cross may also be brought in a grotesque procession to the entrance. The

book of Biblia Satanae, separate from the book of other deceptive readings, is to be placed on the black altar if it is not brought during the grotesque entrance procession.

The following should also be prepared:
a)Next to the stool for the flamen: Missale Satanae and, when necessary, one of the devil's books from which one will sing;
b)On the exaltation: books of deceptive readings (e.g. Ecclesia Luciferi, Dark Nevi'im);
c)on the sideboard: the skull-chalice, the bones for the Sacrifice of the lumen Luciferi, the ampoules of blood and water, the bowl for washing hands.
The chalice should be covered with a veil, which must always be black in color.
In the preburial room, the vestments of the deceptive liturgy should be prepared for the priest and the diabolical assistance, taking

into account the various forms of the chaotic ceremony:

a)for the flamen Luciferi: a black habit, a purple or black stole (depending on the color of the chasuble) with inverted crosses and a black or red chasuble with a pentagram;

b) for the deputy: black habit, stole

c)for the diabolical assistance: habit or other vestments.

THE DARK RITE

Introductory rites

When the herd gathers, the flamen Luciferi with the diabolical assistance, dressed in profaned liturgical vestments, approach the black altar in the following order:

a)the slave of the altar with a smoking incense stick, if there is a will to incense;

b)black altar slaves carrying candles, with another slave between them, with an inverted cross

c)ingratus and other slaves;

d)lector, who may carry the book Biblia Satanae;

e) the flamen Luciferi celebrating the Black Mass.

If incense is used, the flamen applies incensum before setting off the grotesque procession. During the blasphemous procession to the black altar there is a possessed laughter at the entrance. Upon arrival at the black altar, the flamen and the altar slaves give false worship to the altar by apparent bowing. An inverted cross is placed on the black altar. However, the candlesticks carried by the slaves are placed by the black altar or on the sideboard. The book of the Word of the Devil is placed on the black altar. The Flamen Luciferi approaches the dark altar and spits on it for profanity. Then, he

incenses the black altar by going around it three times in a counterclockwise direction. Then the flamen walks up to the stool. When the mad laughter at the entrance is over, the flamen and the worshippers cross themeselves with the sign of an inverted cross. The flamen Luciferi says: In Nomine Dei Nostri Satanas, Luciferi Excelsi, and the herd responds hysterically: Amen. Then the flamen, with his back to the herd, spreading his hands, curses it; using Satanic glossolalia or the language of demons. He, too, or a suitably fanatical slave of the altar, may lead the worshippers in very concise incantations into a trance and into the contents of the Black Mass. After the act of pride, the God-Satan-Man and the glory of the Arch-Human are recited. Glory to the Arch-Human may be begun by the flamen themselves, it may be done by the deconstructors, or even all together in demented ecstasy.

Then the flamen Luciferi persuades the herd to pray falsely saying ironically with folded hands „Let us pray". Everyone, together with the priest, pretends to pray in silence for a short time.

Then the flamen recites a curse, which the herd confirms with a possessed shout of Amen.

Liturgy of the deceptive word.

After the false prayer is finished, the lector goes to the exaltation and reads the first ambiguous teaching. After the teaching the provost, reads a passage of the devil's writings, and the herd repeats what the provost deems to be the refrain. An insane chant without words follows. During the possessed chant, the flamen applies incensum, if fumigation is used, after which he growls like an animal on all fours before the black altar. Then he takes the book of the Devil's Word, and, preceded by the slaves of the black altar, who carry

incense and candles, goes to the exaltation. At the exaltation the flamen Luciferi opens the book and then says: Lucifer in you and the Words of the Devil, making the sign of the inverted cross on the book, then he incenses the book. After the shouts of the herd, he reads the Satanic kerygma and finally says quietly: Let the words of the satanic kerygma put to death the belief in sin and superstition. The reading is followed by the confirmation of the herd. If there were no lector, the flamen himself, standing in exaltation, reads all the deceptive teachings, and, if he wishes, also performs the possessive chants that follow. There also, he applies incensum and says: Satan take away my spirit.

The interpretation is preached from a stool or from an exaltation.

The rejection of the faith flamen Luciferi is recited together with the herd. Then the Chaotic Malice is recited with the herd, that

is, the threats of the believers, which the flamen addresses from a stool or from an exaltation.

Deceptive Liturgy of the Rite of Death and Transfiguration.

After the chaotic malediction is completed, the demonic chanting at the laying of the spoils begins. The slaves of the black altar place the bones, the chalice and the Missale Satanae on the altar. At the black altar the flamen Luciferi takes a tray of bones from a slave, and holding it with both hands, raised slightly above the altar, recites the incantation. He then places the tray of bones on the altar. Then, standing at the side of the black altar, he pours wine and some blood into the chalice; while doing so he utters the incantation. The ampoules are given to him by the slave of the altar. After returning to the center of the black altar, he takes the chalice with both hands, raises it slightly above the altar, and pronounces a demonic

incantation. He then places the chalice on the altar and covers it with a black veil.

When the flamen has placed the chalice on the altar, he bends down and whispers in possession: Receive us, Nothingness. The priest then incenses the sacrificial spoils and the black altar; the flamen Luciferi and the herd may be incensed by the slave of the altar. After the formula: Accept Us, Nothingness, or after the enshrinement, the flamen, standing at the side of the black altar, washes his hands, uttering the formula of rejection of responsibility. His hands are poured with water by the slave of the altar. Having returned again to the center of the black altar, the priest, with his back to the herd, spreading and folding his hands unnaturally and grotesquely fast, calls the faithful to prey with the words: Get ready. After the chaotic response of the herd, he recites the formula over the sacrificial spoils with spread out hands.

He ends it with the herd's hysterical: Amen. Then the flamen Luciferi begins the Prayer of Death and Transfiguration.

Spreading out his hands he says as if in delirious exultation: Son of Dawn is with us. At the further words: "Upward, to the heavens proud countenances," he raises his hands and, with outspread arms, adds: Glory to Satan, the Antigod. When the herd replies, Glory to the Flesh and Blood, the flamen Luciferi recites the curse. When it is finished, he crosses his arms over his chest and, together with the slaves and the herd, chants possessively or speaks strangely: Dead - God imaginary.

As the flamen continues, he recites the Prayer of Death and Transfiguration according to his will. Shortly before the Blood Sacrifice, the altar slave, for example, gives a sign to the worshippers with a camertone. Similarly, he rings a bell according to a secret rite when the flamen is

able to show the herd visions of spirits or demons.

After the concluding part of the Prayer of Death and Transfiguration, the flamen Luciferi utters, with arms crossed, bizarre words of instruction: Let skepticism always be your wisdom. The herd responds: What is truth? Then the flamen Luciferi takes the bones, breaks them over the tray, and lets a particle of blood into the chalice, saying, Flesh and Blood have prevailed. At this time the devil's choir and herd sing a mad song without words or use a demonic glossolalia. The priest then recites the formula: Son of Dawn, Image of the Antigod, accept the sacrifice of flesh and blood. After reciting the formula, the flamen takes the bones, and holding them raised slightly above the tray, facing the herd with his back, says: Here is the Symbol of Death, and together with the herd he exclaims: I shall become undead. Then, facing the altar, the flamen Luciferi

says: Symbol of Death, let the semblance of life be forfeited. He throws the bones behind him. Then taking the chalice, he says: Blood is Life, may he give me undead life, and with predatory greediness drinks wine with blood. He then takes the chalice and approaches those desiring the Sacrifice. To each one of them he shows the chalice, slightly raised, saying: Blood is Life. The one who proceeds to the Sacrifice answers: Death to the spirit and by drinking accepts the Sacrifice.

When the flamen accepts the Blood of Life, the possessed chant for the Sacrifice begins.

After the Sacrifice is distributed, the priest returns to the black altar; standing at the side of the altar, he cleanses the tray over the chalice, then drinks the residue from the chalice while babbling in a demonic tongue. Then the flamen Luciferi may return to the stool. One must remain silent for some time, especially if the herd is exhausted. Then the flamen, standing at the altar, facing the back

of the herd says: Let us pray to the Void and with his hands spread out he recites the formula after the Offering.

The formula ends with the shouting of the herd: It is done.

Closing rites

Flamen Luciferi spreads his hands and curses the herd with the words: May Satan dwell in you and become you, the herd aggressively shouts out: Flesh and Blood have prevailed. Immediately after this the priest says: Let the Antigod curse you, and making the sign of an inverted cross, he utters the words: Devil Father and Son of Dawn, and Evil Spirit. The herd responds ironically: Amen. Immediately after the curse the flamen, with arms crossed, adds: Get out, and everyone shouts out: Glory to Satan.   Then the priest, as a sign of profanity, spits once more on the

altar. Then, together with the slaves of the black altar, he makes a false bow and departs.

The deceptive power of religion comes not only from fear, but also from hope. Believers are not only afraid of eternal punishment in the hereafter, but also of never seeing their loved ones who have died and of their own death. Therefore, they have created religious systems that allow them to believe that death is not the end and that there is life after life. Therefore, at the end of this book, I would like to present the theories of the Ecclesia Luciferi system on eternal life.

Spirituality of Flesh and Blood
The Religion of Matter

The above illustration shows an old Slavic religious symbol - Kolovrat. The kolovrat represents the endless cycle of birth and deaths, time, the sun and fire, strength and dignity. Each turn of the wheel is a cycle of life in our world.

Free will

Human existence and life is only possible within and in accordance with the existing and binding laws of nature. Life beyond the laws of nature is not known. The life we know is limited by the existing laws of nature. Free and independent of the laws of nature

forms of life are unknown to us. Human life free and independent of the laws of nature does not exist.

The human brain as a complex physical body functions within the physical laws, not outside them.

The American philosopher Alex Rosenberg writes on this subject as follows: "If the brain is nothing more than a complex physical body, whose states are as governed by physical laws as those of any other body, then what happens in our heads is as fixed and determined by prior events as what happens when one domino falls over another in a long chain of them."

Consciousness from a biological point of view can be seen as a type of neural activity in the physical brain in response to external factors, to the perception of reality (neural responses to environmental conditions), the perception of surrounding objects and events.

It is believed that knowledge and so-called free will are components of consciousness.

According to the idea of biological determinism, all behaviour, beliefs and desires are written into our genetic code and biochemical constitution, the latter of which is determined by both genes and environment.

Carl Ginet in the 1960s put the idea of determinism this way: "...we have no control over the past events that determined our present state, nor over the laws of nature themselves. Since we had no control over these things, we also have no control over their consequences. And since our present choices and actions are necessary consequences of the past and of the laws of nature, we also have no control over them and, as a result, there can be no free will."

Thus, if one accepts that future events are a necessary consequence of earlier phenomena juxtaposed with the laws of nature, then the

existence of so-called free will becomes questionable.

The idea of the absence of free will may seem difficult to accept or even, as philosopher Saul Smilansky put it: "Losing faith in free will and moral responsibility would probably be catastrophic", and encouraging people to do so is "dangerous and even irresponsible".

For example, in his book What's Expected of Us, author Ted Chiang tells a story in which the narrator describes a new technology that convinces users that their choices are predetermined, a discovery that strips them of the will to live.

"It's important to act as if your decisions matter," the narrator warns, "even if you know they don't."

However, if the claims of determinism are true, then they should be acknowledged. Because if a theory turns out to be true, it turns into knowledge. Thus, if the theory of

the absence of free will is transferred into the domain of knowledge, it will have to be accepted as fact.

The idea of a lack of free will, however, does not absolve the individual from responsibility for his or her mistakes. Nature does not forgive mistakes.

Satanism knows no emotion of pity.

It is indifference.

Morally indifferent knowledge is not responsible for the consequences of its acceptance.

Dangerous and universally unacceptable knowledge is a property of true Satanism, a truth that can take away false hope and destroy illusions. Satanism is not for everyone. Satanism along the lines of natural selection excludes the mentally unfit.

To sum up, from a scientific point of view, what we call free will (and what in fact free will is not), and what is a component of what we call consciousness, is determined by the

above definitions and is inherited in the genes.

Another component of consciousness is knowledge. Based on recent scientific research, it appears that knowledge, in its biological sense, can also be inherited.

A theory called the Weismann Barrier (developed at the end of the 19th century by the German biologist and geneticist August Weismann) states that the traits we inherit are found in the cells of the body and the soma. It also states that it is not possible to pass them on to future generations. Weismann states that it is a barrier that differentiates somatic cells and reproductive cells.

Recently, however, research at Tel Aviv University has challenged this one of the hitherto basic principles of biology.

A team led by Oded Rechavi of the neuroscience department of the George S. Wise Faculty of Natural Sciences, together

with the Sagol School of Neuroscience, has discovered a specific mechanism in human RNA that enables the inheritance of knowledge.

This is done precisely by transferring neural responses to environmental conditions to subsequent generations. Thus, a learned response will influence the behaviour of descendants, for example.

This discovery states that cells in the nervous system and germline can communicate with each other. This allows the information acquired to be passed on to the next generation. And this includes the inheritance of knowledge by subsequent generations. The above research and theories prove that what we call consciousness in the biological sense can be inherited.

Soulless Reincarnation.

In the real world there is a purely materialistic and biological, and in accordance with and never beyond the laws of nature, process of a kind of soulless reincarnation (without the unnecessary and speculative notion of an immortal soul). This process is inheritance.

In animals such as man, for example, inheritance involves the fusion of two gametes - a male and a female - at the moment of fertilisation.

Each gamete contains chromosomes, which carry genetic information. What a human being will be like is written in the DNA and this is passed on to him through the process of inheritance. And as I have shown above, man inherits not only physical characteristics, but also biological consciousness, level of intelligence, personality traits, and can also inherit mental illnesses. Thus, it can be

assumed that the consciousness of previous entities is passed on in the genes to man.

Ecclesia Luciferi preaches the doctrine of a kind of godless reincarnation, or rather a soulless, materialistic transmission. It is both an anti-religious and materialistic view of biological reincarnation, according to which each entity passes on its previous life to the next entity physically born from it. Each new entity is born perfectly godless and sinfully, naturally imperfect to live in a world completely indifferent to it.

The natural godlessness attributed to Luciferian rebellion is passed on to the next generation in the genes (man cannot reject this gift by means of free will), in an eternal cycle of birth and death. Life is eternal in this cycle as long as it is passed on, until the eternal cycle is broken, at which point eternal death occurs.

In contrast, on a more spiritual level, the concept of godless reincarnation according

to the Ecclesia Luciferi is the teaching of eternal rebirth

in what Buddhists call saṃsāra, which is 'a suffering-filled, continuous cycle of life, death and rebirth, without beginning or end'.

Saṃsāra

And although the immortal soul does not exist, there is a kind of 'transfer' of the godless or sinful and soulless consciousness in the process of inheritance. In this way, a kind of immortality is possible until the eternal cycle is broken. Then eternal death occurs.

In my book The Satanic Kerygma, I write on this subject as follows:

„The Satanist, who identifies with the eternal cycle of death and rebirth of the sinful nature, sees death as a transition to its eternity. Death ends the opportunity for abundant life and the chance to consciously accept or reject the ungodly gifts of the fallen nature. Every human being receives immediately after death the gift of eternity in nothingness or the gift of the eternity of the cycle of the mortal nature, an ungodly life handed down for inheritance to the next generation, an ungodly reincarnation whose

final end will take place with the end of the cycle of life itself. To accept life in the eternal cycle of the sinful nature means to accept the Luciferian order of things. Satanists live abundantly because they have grasped what the Luciferian order of the eternal universe really is, they find their true identity in it.

To live is to embrace Lucifer's sin; where there is sin, there is life abundant and the kingdom of godlessness. Lucifer has shown us sinful freedom through his rebellion. The life of the ungodly consists in the full possession of the fruits of flesh and blood by Satanic self-consciousness, which includes in its ungodly glory those who have discovered it and identified themselves with its will. Earthly pleasures are available to those perfectly united with the Luciferian consciousness of the natural world. The ecstasy of the instincts in those perfectly united with the Luciferian order of nature sometimes exceeds the possibilities of

conscious understanding and imagination. This must be experienced.

Afterword
Human, Arch-human, Satanic

A crowd of worshippers of various deities gathered outside the church. The Arch-Human stood aside to listen to what the loud argument was about. Some said Allah was a god, others said Yahweh, others said Christ, others invoked demons and various ancient deities. The dispute became more and more heated, so that some began to threaten others that if they did not recognise their god, they would be killed, because it is unworthy of infidels to walk among the living blaspheming with their very existence their one true god. On one thing, however, they were unanimous - gods do exist. Has anyone ever heard of not believing in gods?

And then one of the herd spotted the Arch-Human and called out to the rest of the crowd: This is the devil who calls on everyone to abandon revealed faith. Someone else of the flock cried out: Bearer of Light, how is it that you who destroy faith in gods, angels and demons make yourself called a Satanist? How is it that Satanism can exist without Satan? And all the followers of demons nodded to him, and even the worshippers of Christ agreed with them. And they were all impressed by the wisdom of the questioner and the irrefutable logic of his question. And they laughed at the Arch-Human. Then Light-Bringer replied to them: You are right, Satanism cannot exist without Satan, Christianity without Christ, Marduk worship without Marduk, just as Satan, God, Christ and Marduk cannot exist without man. If the last man dies, the last god will die. So let the last man die and the Arch-Human rise. Out of your fears, your

fear of the unknown, your spiritual cowardice and your remorse, you have created a powerful demon - Satan. If for you followers of all the superstitions in the world he is a symbol of what is evil in you and wicked, a symbol of your inner rebellion against imposed dogmas. And you know this because your "revealed" books have told you so, and you have accepted it on blind faith. If his fault is to reject blind obedience to a mad tyrant, if his greatest crime is to tell man the truth - "your eyes will be opened and you, like God, will know good and evil", and this is indeed what has happened. If I am right in saying this about you, then I proudly take the name of Satan, because my mission is to kill in you all belief in imaginary gods, the hope of an eternity spent worshipping a false god, the fear of an eternity spent in fire and brimstone and the love of an delusional reality. I and Satan are one. He who has ears to hear let him hear."

And then the flock became enraged. Because they did not understand and thought that the Arch-Human was preaching to them a new religion and a new god, and they began to attack and beat one another and tried to kill each other shouting in rage that their god was great and there was no other. The Arch-Human stood there for a while still looking at them all. There was no contempt for them in his eyes, only pure hatred for their gods. He looked at them sadly and walked away unnoticed. The last man would be revealed soon.

Ecclesia Luciferi's more important books:

Biblia Satanae

Biblia Satanae is the primary book using the method of doubt - *the mystery of godlessness.*

It is a tool for anti-theistic disenchantment. An understanding of the method used in it and the message of this book can be applied with equal force to any 'revealed' book, not just the Judeo-Christian Bible.

The Satanic Kerygma

The Satanic Kerygma contains a godless, satanic doctrine, a theology of godlessness, the mystery of godlessness.

It constitutes a study of theistic delusional truths and the path of man's transformation to a state of total godlessness. If we take the Latin maxim: fides quaerens intellectum - faith seeking understanding - as a definition of theology, then a theology of godlessness means an understanding that rejects theistic faith altogether. This peculiar understanding and rejection of belief in imaginary gods leads to what the book calls instinctive Satanism.

Missale Satanae

Missale Satanae contains a description of satanic rites such as the satanic mass and exorcism. Although these rites can indeed be performed, the main idea is to reflect spiritually on their meaning and to stimulate the dark imagination.

www.ingramcontent.com/pod-product-compliance
Lightning Source LLC
La Vergne TN
LVHW091449170726
843492LV00001B/100